THE BEATLES

THE BEATLES

TEXT BY
GEOFFREY STOKES

INTRODUCTION BY
LEONARD BERNSTEIN

ART DIRECTION BY
BEA FEITLER

Times BOOKS

Rolling Stone

A Rolling Stone Press Book
Published by Times Books, a division of Quadrangle/The New York Times Book Co., Inc.
Three Park Avenue, New York, N.Y. 10016.
Published simultaneously in Canada by Fitzhenry & Whiteside, Ltd., Toronto.

Library of Congress Cataloging in Publication Data
Stokes, Geoffrey.

The Beatles.
"A Rolling Stone Press book."
1. Beatles. 2. Rock musicians—England—
Biography. I. Title.
ML421.B4S76   784.5′4′00922 [B]   80-5138
ISBN 0-8129-0928-3
ISBN 0-8129-1007-9 PBK.

Manufactured in the United States of America.

I really thought that love would save us all.

[JOHN]

ACKNOWLEDGMENTS

Since virtually everybody who ever knew the Beatles felt compelled
to commit their memories to print, research for this book was both easy and exhausting.
Among the most useful of these many memoirs were Michael Braun's *Love Me Do*
Brian Epstein's *A Cellarful of Noise*, Derek Taylor's *As Time Goes By*, and
Allan Williams's *The Man Who Gave the Beatles Away*. The collected issues of
Mersey Beat provided an invaluable sense of the Liverpool scene, but as one might expect,
the boys always spoke best for themselves. Barry Miles's collection,
Beatles in Their Own Words was a helpful compendium, and *Lennon Remembers*
remains a landmark among interviews.
There were, of course, objective reports as well. Among the outsiders,
Hunter Davies's 1968 *The Beatles* though authorized and Bowdlerized, is also evocative
and factual; Peter McCabe's and Robert D. Schonfeld's *Apple to the Core* is the
definitive account of the Beatles' disintegration. Of the books that attempt to
combine historiography and criticism, Nicholas Schaffner's *The Beatles Forever*
provides reliable fact and plausible criticism. And critics Greil Marcus and
Robert Christgau have most compellingly "explained" the Beatles;
their insights inform this work throughout.
The editors of this book would like to express special thanks to Ron Furmanek
for his help and advice. Most of the memorabilia and many photographs came from
his unique archives of Beatles material. We are indebted to him.
A number of people also contributed their time and effort specifically to this book.
Those who should share any praise — and escape all blame — include
Jackson Brader, Maureen Cleave, Peter Collins, Jonathan Cott, Robert Freeman,
Paul Gambaccini, Larry Goldman, Alan Grebowski, Dezo Hoffmann, Marvin Israel,
John Kosh, Donna Lucey, Thom Mount, Michele Napear, Sean O'Mahoney,
Brian Southall, Ralph Steadman, and Al Steckler.

INTRODUCTION

Once, a year ago (four years ago? last month?), I was asked by *Rolling Stone* to write a 5000-word introduction to a definitive volume on the Beatles —not the, but *The* Beatles. I instantly assented; but that was then, and today is fraught, and these several words must replace, inadequately, alas, what an introduction ought to do.

I fell in love with the Beatles' music (and simultaneously, of course, with their four faces-cum-personae) along with my children, two girls and a boy, in whom I discovered the frabjous falsetto shriek-cum-croon, the ineluctable beat, the flawless intonation, the utterly fresh lyrics, the Schubert-like flow of musical invention and the Fuck-You coolness of these Four Horsemen of Our Apocalypse, on the *Ed Sullivan Show* of 1964. Jamie was then twelve, Alexander nine, and Nina two. Together we saw it, The Vision, in our inevitably different ways (I was forty-six!), but we saw the same Vision, and heard the same Dawn-Bird, Elephant-Trump, Fanfare of the Future. What Future? Here we are, fifteen years later, and it's all gone. But for a decade or so, or even less, it remained the same Vision-Clarion, yet increasingly cogent, clear, bitter —and better.

Perhaps the clearest, bitterest (and maybe best) was an album called *Revolver* (*pace Sgt. Pepper, Abbey Road, et al.*). Of this album, perhaps the very best was a little-known ditty called "She Said She Said," the very thought and memory of which recalls all the beauty of those Vietnamese Varicose Veins. The notes healed, the words teased; or perhaps it was vice versa. But *something* teased, and something healed, year after year, Rigby after Rigby, Paperback after Norwegian, perhaps ultimately signified in the gleaming, dreary truth of "She's Leaving Home."

Meanwhile, there was a slim volume of pure verbal genius by a new author called *John Lennon: In His Own Write*. If this weren't enough to rhapsodize upon, there were the notes (and the sylph-siren voice) of one McCartney. These two made a pair embodying a creativity mostly unmatched during that fateful decade. Ringo — a lovely performer. George — a mystical unrealized talent. But John and Paul, Saints John and Paul, were, and made, and aureoled and beatified and eternalized the concept that shall always be known, remembered and deeply loved as The Beatles.

And yet, the two were merely something, the four were It. The interdependence was astonishing, and in some ways appalling; do we really need all this to sustain us When We're 64? Well, today I am almost 64, and three bars of "A Day in the Life" still sustain me, rejuvenate me, inflame my senses and sensibilities.

Nina, who was two way back then in '64, is now seventeen; and only last week we took out that thick, wretched Beatles volume of ill-printed sheet music and reminisced at the piano. We wept, we jumped with the joy of recognition ("She's a Woman") — just the two of us, for hours ("Ticket to Ride," "A Hard Day's Night," "I Saw Her Standing There") . . .

That was last week. The Beatles are no more. But this week I am still jumping, weeping, remembering a good epoch, a golden decade, a fine time, a fine time . . .   *LEONARD BERNSTEIN/October 9th, 1979*

THE BEATLES

"THE FIRST THING WE DID WAS TO PROCLAIM OUR LIVERPOOLNESS TO THE WORLD, AND SAY 'IT'S ALL RIGHT TO COME FROM LIVERPOOL AND TALK LIKE THIS.'" — John Lennon

Teenagers everywhere seek the new; in drab, gray Liverpool, ten years after World War II, they demanded it. The sense of common purpose that had linked that Northern port with London during the Nazi threat had by then evaporated, and with the restoration of the Conservative government, England had gone very much back to normal.

"Normal" Liverpool was an outpost of Tory provincialism whose theater groups and proper restaurants were embarrassed imitations of London's. But there was another city as well: Welsh, Irish, working-class, Labour and chapel. Finally, it was international, for Liverpool's dockside streets echoed with the accents of visiting sailors. This singing, brawling mixture produced a culture that was not so much provincial as alien.

Even its music stood apart from London's, and "Maggie May," a bawdy tribute to an archetypal Lime Street prostitute, was this Liverpool's swaggering anthem. But the shifting crowd of American sailors who supported Maggie's sisters carried their own music with them as well, and working-class Liverpool sprouted dozens of clubs devoted to blues and country music where local performers sported sequined suits under their imported Stetsons.

These show bands—with their note-for-note recreations of records brought in by American seamen—were Liverpool's primary source of musical information. The British Broadcasting Corporation had grudgingly embraced Tin Pan Alley, but working-class Liverpool—perhaps recognizing a kindred spirit—embraced America's "other" musics.

The jubilant American invention called rock 'n' roll swept this Liverpool with a force that left London irrelevant. Among teenagers there was no contest; rock 'n' roll was their lover, their saviour, their escape. For them, shocking the proper wasn't so much a political act as a recklessly joyful self-definition. And if the definition was shared by a whole generation, then the kids were all right: One rebel is caned; two are outcasts; thousands are a culture. When Bill Haley's "Rock around the Clock" stormed onto the British charts in July 1955, John and Ringo were fourteen, Paul thirteen and George twelve.

John had by then been providing his share of shocks to the family for some time. He was born in the fall of 1940, with Liverpool under heavy bombing, and his father, Fred Lennon, at sea as a merchant seaman. Shortly thereafter Fred Lennon was no longer at sea, but in jail for desertion. Though he was released in only a few months, John's mother had already found a new man and had sent John to live with her married sister, Mimi Smith. Firmly established on the lower rungs of the ladder to respectability, Uncle George managed the family milk-delivery business, while Aunt Mimi managed John. Or tried to.

Despite Mimi's efforts—and an innate fascination with words that started him writing "books" at the age of eight—John distinguished himself in grammar school chiefly through his fists. He led a gang of fledgling

Preceding pages: "Liverpool? You're joking. So what's from Liverpool?" asked music publisher when told about a new group called the Beatles.

4

toughs in shoplifting, hitching rides on trolleys, and harassing girls. Nevertheless, he managed to get into Quarry Bank High School, a still-respectable institution near Mimi's home. During his first year, a teacher discovered him making obscene drawings and young John was tagged as a troublemaker—a badge he wore with increasing pride and stubbornness. By his second year, when he was thirteen, his report card read, "Hopeless. Rather a clown in class. He is just wasting other pupils' time." During that year his Uncle George died, and Mimi slipped a bit down the ladder and began taking boarders. It was at this time that John's mother reentered his life.

Julia Lennon cheerfully defied the conventions that held her sister in thrall. She loved an audience, and in John and his rowdy friends she found an adoring one. Rather than condemning his adolescent acts of rebellion, as Mimi felt she should, Julia used her visits to egg him on. (A friend of John's remembers Julia once walking solemnly down a crowded street with her underwear on her head.) It was Julia who bought John his first guitar and taught him a few chords she'd learned on the banjo.

The guitar came along with the skiffle craze —the mania for jug-band music that swept all England in the mid-Fifties. Skiffle king Lonnie Donegan produced more number-one hits during 1956 and '57 than archrival Elvis Presley. Donegan's pseudo-American accent propelled "Rock Island Line" and eight other records onto the British charts, offering a casual, shuffling music far easier to imitate than Presley's amplified professionalism. Skiffle, with its washboards and one-string basses, was, like rock 'n' roll, an af-front to conventional pop. *Anybody*, it seemed, could play skiffle. And almost everybody did.

Early in 1956, John, armed with his new guitar, recruited classmates to form the Quarrymen, thus beginning his musical career.

Though they lived in the government-funded council housing, Jim and Mary Patricia McCartney had a tenuous grip on respectability. Jim had left school at age fourteen to work as a sample boy for a cotton broker, but later became a salesman who wore a white collar to work; Mary Patricia was a trained nurse-midwife. They had ambitions for their children—wanted them to go to University—and their older boy, Paul, seemed likely to fulfill their dreams.

When he began high school at Liverpool Institute, Paul did quite well, but soon felt the gap between his council-house friends and his parents' dreams. He began adapting to local mores—shoplifting, smoking—but his natural intelligence and gift for written words enabled him to keep pace at school. Then, in 1956, when Paul was fourteen, his mother died of cancer.

The blow was twofold. In addition to the enormous emotional shock, her death crippled the family financially. The cotton trade had, by then, slacked off enough so that she'd been earning more money than her husband; he was left with two teenage boys to raise on his own salary of only £8 a week. But somehow he managed to put together £15 to buy a guitar for Paul.

Paul had fooled around with music before his mother's death and had taught himself to play the trumpet. There always was music in the McCartney home; until the boys were

born, Jim moonlighted playing piano at local dances in his own band. But Paul didn't like dance-hall music; like most of his generation, he was seduced by skiffle. The craze hit when he was fourteen, and he recalls spending a lunch hour standing outside a theater to catch a glimpse of Lonnie Donegan. By then, the left-handed McCartney had learned to string the guitar upside down and could pick out Elvis' chords when Presley began to shoulder Donegan from the charts.

Paul immersed himself in all kinds of American rock (his versions of Little Richard survive on early Beatles records). Though never a full-fledged "Ted," he began adopting their street-fighter style—tightening his trousers into the classic Teddy Boy "drainies" and primping his hair into a Tony Curtis pompadour. From the ashes of his mother's death, he created a new Paul—a guitar-picking swaggerer whose chief interest was no longer University, but girls. He went to hear the Quarrymen playing at the Woolton Parish Church because he hoped he could pluck a girl from their audience.

'Julia' is the song of love John wrote about his mother (left). Although raised by his Aunt Mimi, John felt his mother understood him best. When she died he said, "It was the worst thing that ever happened to me." Above: John at nine

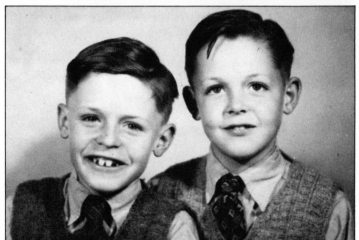

Instead, Paul met John. In Hunter Davies' authorized biography, Paul recalls getting together with the Quarrymen after that performance. "I showed them how to play 'Twenty Flight Rock' and told them all the words . . . I remember this beery old man getting nearer and breathing down my neck as I was playing. 'What's this old drunk doing?' I thought. Then he said 'Twenty Flight Rock' was one of his favorites. So I knew he was a connoisseur."

About a week later, through a mutual friend, the dirty old connoisseur invited Paul into the group. The delay occurred partly because they went to different schools, but also because John had to decide whether he

When Paul was born, his father wept at the sight of him. "He looked so horrible and squawked all the time," and yet "he turned out a lovely baby in the end." Left: Paul with his mother Mary Patricia and brother Michael. Above: Both boys, 7 and 9, and their council house

wanted to join up with someone who could play guitar as well as he did—and maybe better. Within a month or two, they had begun writing songs with each other—silly love songs, mostly, with a heavy flavor of Buddy Holly, but the chemistry was right. The

Quarrymen, though they didn't know it, were on their way to becoming the Beatles.

The unamplified acoustic sound and primitive technique remained skiffle-ish, but the material was influenced much more by rock 'n' roll. The change was to some extent a matter of personal inclination; after all, the first song John taught himself to pick all the way through on the guitar had been Buddy Holly's "That'll Be the Day." But it was also a reaction to the dissolution of the English folkie scene. Coincident with Holly's emergence, the music was going through the crisis of "relevance" that would split American folkies seven years later. One branch was trying to keep folk tradition alive by writing new songs in centuries-old modes, while the

His mother said George was a willing little boy who would just "hop behind the chair and give you a puppet show whenever you asked." Top: George's house on Macketts Lane. Above: George, 8, with his family. Right: George at five

10

more sprightly skifflers sang only traditional songs. Each group, however, was pumping a dry well, and neither had anything at all to say to post-Presley Liverpool teenagers. Thus when Paul, after a little more than a year with the Quarrymen, brought a younger school friend to try out for the group, George Harrison auditioned by playing an American rock 'n' roll instrumental, "Raunchy."

John and Paul, living out their overlapping fantasies, were pseudotough; George was the real thing. Before finally getting a job as a bus conductor, his father had been on welfare for more than a year; his mother chipped in with her earnings as a part-time clerk at a local fruit-and-vegetable stand. Of their four children, George was the only one to survive the schools' weeding-out process and go on, entering Liverpool Institute a year behind Paul. But, more interested in clothes than

school, he was remarkable chiefly for his tight jeans and his "Scouse" speech. He was hard-core low-Liverpool—no Aunt Mimi had ever labored over his accent.

Though the Harrisons never had much money, they always tried to help, and when George fell under the influence of Lonnie Donegan, his mother found £3 to buy him his first guitar. She also stayed up late, encouraging him when he thought he'd never learn to play it.

Measured against the upwardly mobile standards of the other Beatles' families, the Harrisons seemed unthreatened by George's fascination with music; though they wanted him to work harder in school, they recognized his increasing musical skill for the accomplishment it was. Still, even they were a bit startled when his explorations into rock 'n' roll made his first guitar obsolete. But once he convinced them that he really needed an electric instrument, they spent £30 to get him one on an installment plan.

He played it incessantly, abandoning schoolwork and losing himself in music. For John, music was just one more outlet for the angry

Above: Ringo's row house (marked by a V over the door) in the Dingle section of Liverpool. "There's a lot of tenements in the Dingle," he said, "a lot of people in little boxes trying to get out." Far left: Ringo's mother Elsie with his stepfather Harry Graves. Left: Ringo with his Mum and the neighbor who taught him to read.

talent he was spilling across his canvases at art school; for Paul, it was a way to redefine himself after the shattering experience of his mother's death. For George, music *was*.

Still, there remained some doubt whether he would fit into the Quarrymen. John was exploring *la vie bohème* at Liverpool Art College, and George was a wiry, gap-toothed, 15-year-old Ted. But he could play—even better than Paul—and with the guitar in his hands, he belonged. By taking him in, Paul and John acknowledged that a proper command of music meant a lot more than a proper accent. With him, the Beatles were three-quarters formed.

In 1958, the year George became a Quarryman, the charts overflowed with a wonderfully exuberant (and somewhat mindless) music that went right to the teenage heart. Buddy Holly had four songs—including "Rave On" and "Peggy Sue"—on the British charts that year; the Everly Brothers had two; Fats Domino, Little Richard and Jerry Lee Lewis, one apiece, and Elvis, six. But in that year a counterrevolution also began, as Cliff Richard, England's answer to Pat Boone, made the first of his many trips to the charts.

Without question, the Quarrymen knew which side they were on. They felt nothing but contempt for the polite, and ever-so-religious, Richard. Rock 'n' roll—*their* music —wasn't polite, wasn't safe, wasn't anything the BBC's darling was. But that didn't stop them from stealing one of his band's riffs when Paul saw them play it on television, and this eclectic embrace of alien styles was to become a hallmark of the Beatles.

As 1958 chugged along, the Quarrymen—by now John, Paul, George and whoever else was available—slowly improved enough to get occasional paying jobs. Very occasional—and George drifted away from school to become an apprentice electrician. His newly acquired trade helped them obtain amplifiers, and they soon left skiffle entirely behind. They were a rock band. But with no bass, and no drummer.

The drummer was a continuing problem, mostly because, as John recalls, "people who owned drum kits were few and far between; it was an expensive item," but an answer—of sorts—to the bass question emerged from among John's cronies at art college. Of the self-consciously rebellious art students hang-

Rock 'n' roll will be whatever we make it.
[JOHN]

ing about in rented Liverpool flats, Stuart Sutcliffe was arguably the most talented. He was also a music fan and spent large stretches of his non-painting time around the developing band. When one of Sutcliffe's paintings won a £60 purchase prize at the prestigious John Moore show, he was persuaded to spend the money on a bass guitar. Though he couldn't play it, he immediately became a member of the band.

George provided Stuart's formal instruction, but the bulk of his musical education came from on-the-job training. Many of those who saw the band during its days as Johnny and the Moondogs—the connection with Quarry Bank High School being long gone—thought of the handsome Sutcliffe as an enigmatic James Dean sort of figure. This image was reinforced by his habit of keeping his back to the crowd during performances—a habit which had less to do with mysteriousness than with his justified embarrassment at being able to play only the most rudimentary patterns.

Still, it was Sutcliffe who introduced Allan Williams to the band. Williams, a hard-drinking figure who flourished on the fringes of Liverpool's rough-and-tumble night life, operated a coffee bar called the Jacaranda Club. The Jac, which offered its customers bacon sandwiches, coffee and a West Indian steel band, was a hangout for Liverpool's proto-hippies, including, naturally enough, Stuart Sutcliffe and John Lennon. Largely through Stuart's influence, Williams allowed the band to practice in his cellar during the afternoon. He provided occasional sandwiches and, since their money was always short, once even hired them to clean and repaint the women's bathroom.

Gradually their afternoon practice sessions turned into gigs, as occasional students wandered down the cellar stairs to listen. Williams thus found himself operating the first of Liverpool's "beat clubs" (the more famous Cavern Club would not convert from jazz to rock 'n' roll until later), and began acting as the band's de facto manager, getting them occasional dance hall dates and taking a small percentage of their fees. He also found them their first more or less regular drummer, Tommy Moore.

Moore, at twenty-five, was an old man (George was only seventeen, and even John was still technically a full-time student).

Nevertheless, he accompanied them on their first non-Liverpool tour; as the Silver Beatles, the band opened for one Johnny Gentle in ballrooms in the far north of Scotland.

They had wanted to be simply "The Beatles," modeling themselves after Buddy Holly's Crickets, but a better-established Liverpool musician (Cass, of Cass and the Casanovas) thought John's role as the band's leader should be highlighted—hence, the Silver Beatles, an obscure reference to Long John Silver. This was certainly in the Liverpool tradition established by Cass's band, Rory Storm and the Hurricanes, Derry and the Seniors, and Gerry and the Pacemakers. The Beatles themselves had adopted it during their days as Johnny and the Moondogs, but their new name meant something else; they were equal, and they were one.

On this tour to Scotland—the first lengthy escape from Liverpool for any of them—they had their first taste of life on their own. Paul sent back a postcard saying, "It's gear. I got asked for my autograph." But they didn't get asked back, and their return to Liverpool found them still distant from stardom. Moore, unable to survive on his meager share of their earnings, took his drums and went back to his steady job driving a forklift at the Garston Bottle Works, and the survivors found themselves playing (among other things, "A Long Way to Tipperary") at a grotty strip club that Williams ran as a sideline. Even there, they were not big hits—the regular customers complained that the boys' music interfered with their fantasies. And they still had no regular drummer.

Following pages: George with his first guitar, and Ringo, 15, a barman on the Mersey River ferry, here taking a break with a chum.

A guitar's all right, John, but you'll never earn your living by it.

[AUNT MIMI]

They did have a part-time one, however. On nights when they played at the Casbah, a suburban coffee bar run by Mrs. Johnny Best, her son Pete sat in with them. Handsome and somewhat sullen, he was known as a competent drummer, but since the chemistry seemed wrong, he was never asked formally to join the group. Still, when Williams lined up a job for them in Hamburg, Pete Best was available. Fifteen pounds a week seemed a lot at the time, so when Paul asked him to join, he did.

Williams had been lured to Hamburg a year earlier, when the Jac's West Indian steel band began sending him glowing reports from their new venue. Nothing had come of his trip, however, until 1960, when he again

Left: John, 15, on one of his first gigs with a band in 1956. "I wanted to be the leader," he said. "I wanted everybody else to do what I told them, to laugh at my jokes and let me be the boss." Above: The Quarrymen later that year, when Paul had joined the group.

met Bruno Koschmider, the owner of the Kaiserkeller, who was in England looking for a rock band to play in his Hamburg club. A booking for Derry and the Seniors, one of Williams' groups, had just been cancelled and he was desperate to find another gig. The fast-talking Williams convinced Koschmider to book the disappointed Derry, who thus became the first Liverpool rock group to play Hamburg. They tore the place up—business was so good that Koschmider promptly decided to open another club, turning again to Liverpool and Williams for entertainment. Gerry and the Pacemakers weren't interested, and Rory Storm and the Hurricanes (Ringo Starr on drums) were already booked into a summer resort, so the job went to the Beatles. Because a West Indian steel band once went to Hamburg . . . because Williams followed them . . . because a booking for Derry and the Seniors was cancelled . . . because Koschmider was in England . . . because Derry did good business for him . . . the Beatles made the move that changed their lives forever.

————————————

The Beatles arrived in Hamburg in the fall of 1960, after a van trip across Holland made all too interesting by Williams' difficulty remembering to drive on the right side of the road. Herr Koschmider greeted them enthusiastically, but did not wax overgenerous in providing the rooms required by their contract. He gave them three long-abandoned dressing rooms behind the screen of a movie house, furnished with a few folding cots. But they decided to put up with the inconvenience when they reached Koschmider's new club, the Indra, and saw the small sign billing them as "The Fabulous Beatles from Liverpool, England."

Their time at the Indra was not a success. Visions of deutsche marks dancing in his head, Koschmider had hurriedly converted it from a strip club. He'd also left the change in policy unadvertised. Customers who expected a Hamburg-style sex show and instead got the not-so-fabulous four were not happy. Since the Beatles' contract had five weeks to go, Koschmider moved them into the larger and more established Kaiserkeller, where they alternated sets with Derry and the Seniors.

At the Kaiserkeller, they blossomed. It was a rough place, the boot and the knife always a menacing presence, but the crowds were ready for rock 'n' roll. They were, in fact, more ready than the Beatles. At home the band's shows had lasted an hour at most; at the Kaiserkeller, they were expected to play at least six times longer. On their first night, though they stretched out their numbers with primitive instrumental bridges, they ran out of material. In a strange city, with no protective adults hovering in the background, in a club where the sound of fist against flesh was the most familiar noise, they had to perform or flee. They expanded their repertoire in a big hurry, singing whatever songs they agreed they all knew, often for the first time together. These were the classics of rock 'n' roll.

They played Buddy Holly, the Everly Brothers, Little Richard, Carl Perkins, Conway Twitty, the Fleetwoods, Duane Eddy, and, of course, Chuck Berry. When they didn't know all the words, they faked them, often dragging in other songs wholesale over their own improvised melodies. On a tiny stage in Hamburg, sweating with fear and excitement, they reinvented rock 'n' roll. They were of its first generation—the only one in which the emotional explosions of puberty had coincided with the music revolution called rock 'n' roll; in Hamburg they charged these Proustian sounds of the Fifties with the hard-edged anger of lower-class Liverpool

and a boy's-night-out exuberance that was all their own.

They couldn't have discovered this style in Liverpool. There, they all lived with their families. They might go out and play all night, but when the music stopped, they returned to domestic life. In Hamburg, the party never ended.

Their Hamburg stays were not the sort of thing parents imagine when they send their children off for a junior year abroad. The Beatles were tough Liverpool teenagers but even they were a little stunned by Hamburg. Leather, whips, mud-wrestling, cruising

transvestites, pistol-packing waiters, all seen through a haze of drink and amphetamines, formed their education. They loved it. Constantly raising each other's bets, they reached deeper and deeper into excess.

Still, every night they roared onto Koschmider's stage to play music that was as thrillingly out of control as they were. Their six-week stay was extended, and extended again. Word about them began to spread, and for the first time they began to draw a different crowd.

Klaus Voormann was the first of the new fans. A commercial artist and important figure among Hamburg's beatnik intelligentsia, he wandered into the Kaiserkeller after a fight with his girlfriend. Like most of his friends, he was a jazz buff, usually avoiding rock 'n' roll as a matter of taste and Koschmider's club as a matter of prudence. Much later that night, he climbed the stairs to the street a Beatles fan. He came back again, alone at first, then with his girlfriend, Astrid Kirchherr. She was a photographer who fell in almost instant visual love with the five tough Teds. She and Klaus approached them, becoming tentative friends. Klaus and Astrid began bringing other students to hear this primitive music, and soon the Kaiserkeller was no longer the sole preserve of leather-jacketed rockers. The new crowd was, in Paul's careful words, "a change from the usual fat Germans." Pete didn't like them, but George, whose background left him to-

Left: Stuart Sutcliffe, art student, was persuaded by John to buy a bass he couldn't play and join the group. "I looked up to Stuart," said John. "I depended on him to tell me the truth the way I do with Paul today. Stu would tell me if something was good and I'd believe him." Overleaf: The Silver Beatles' audition that led to their first tour. Stuart is at left. Johnny Hutch stood in as a last-minute drummer.

tally unprepared for a bohemian life style, was perpetually astonished and halfway infatuated. He thought the arty types were "really groovy."

Astrid took their pictures, and the boys—except for Pete—began eating what passed for their regular nightly meal at her house. She and Stuart began an affair, fell in love, and two months later became engaged.

And then during a break one night, the Beatles wandered around the corner to sit in with Tony Sheridan at the Top Ten Club, Koschmider's biggest competitor. He was furious and they promised to be good lads but, in what all concerned claim was an accident involving an inflamed condom-rocket, they set fire to their backstage rooms.

Koschmider, biting off his nose to spite his face, complained to the police, and the Beatles' first Hamburg tour came to a sudden and inglorious end. George and Paul, underage and without work permits, were formally deported; the others got home as best they could. They didn't play together, or even meet, for a while, and Paul, whose father got him a factory job, wasn't the only one to think the Beatles were finished.

Brian Kelly is one of the handful of people who can lay plausible claim to the title of The Man Who Discovered the Beatles, and from time to time has done so. A minor Liverpool promoter, Kelly was organizing a Boxing Day show to be held in nearby Litherland on December 27th, 1960, when he got a call from Bob Wooler, a DJ and perhaps the major Liverpool force in popularizing American rock 'n' roll. As Kelly recalled the conversation, it began with Wooler saying, "I've found a group for you at the Jacaranda, and

they're free. They want £8. Will they do?"

"Not at that price, they won't," said Kelly. After a sales pitch from Wooler, he finally agreed to £6. He got considerably more than he bargained for.

These Beatles were nothing like the pre-Hamburg band. They were still scruffy Teds, but they had developed a full-throttle style of performing that captured the attention of Liverpool so thoroughly that their Litherland Town Hall appearance sparked a screaming, stomping riot. This was the first of many, and Kelly quickly took advantage of it; as soon as their show ended, he surrounded their dressing room with his bouncers, barring all other promoters until he had talked with the band. By the time he left, the Beatles had signed on for a lengthy series of Kelly's promotions—at £8 a night.

At each of Kelly's shows, and in the dozens of other venues where they performed, the reaction was the same. By early 1961, the Beatles were *stars*! But only on a very local level. They worked hard, they drew crowds, they got paid as much as £3 each for a night's show, but they weren't, they felt, *going* anywhere; two pounds here, three there, and they'd still wind up with less than they'd earn driving a forklift. By comparison, Hamburg looked very good indeed.

As it happened, work was waiting for them there. Peter Eckhorn, a relatively reputable sort who operated the Top Ten Club, wanted to hire the Beatles. There was, however, the unfortunate matter of their deportation. Once again, Allan Williams intervened, writing a letter to the German Consul in Liverpool in which he blamed the missing work permits on Koschmider. He further stretched the truth by solemnly proclaiming that "all the musicians have very good characters and come from first-class families and they have never been in trouble with the police in this country." For reasons that perhaps had more to do with Eckhorn's discreet prodding in the home country than Williams' prose, the Consul agreed to issue work permits. In April 1961, George having turned eighteen, the Beatles left local fame—and local wages—to earn £150 a week at Eckhorn's Top Ten Club.

The Top Ten was much larger than the Kaiserkeller, but despite the number of students attracted by the Beatles, just about as rough. The work, too, was exhausting: six or seven hours of music every night, with fifteen-minute breaks at the end of each hour. In no time, educated by their last Hamburg trip, they were back on pills—mixed with the large quantities of drink that their fans bought for them. Cynthia Powell, who spent

Upper left: John and Paul at a Liverpool club; Cynthia Powell, John's future wife, looks on. Above: On the way to Hamburg the Beatles pose at Arnhem War Memorial. Tour organizer Allan Williams is at left, Stu is wearing sunglasses, drummer Pete Best, hired for the tour, is at right. Following pages: 1961, Paul and George

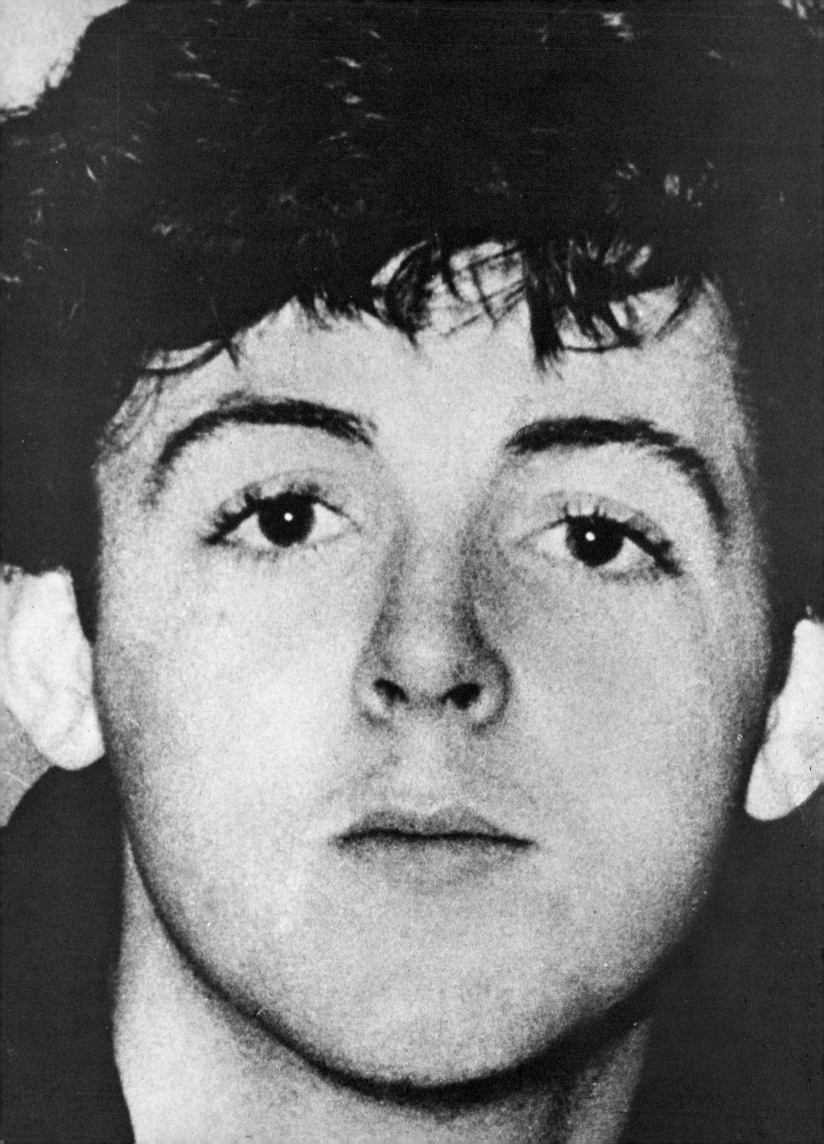

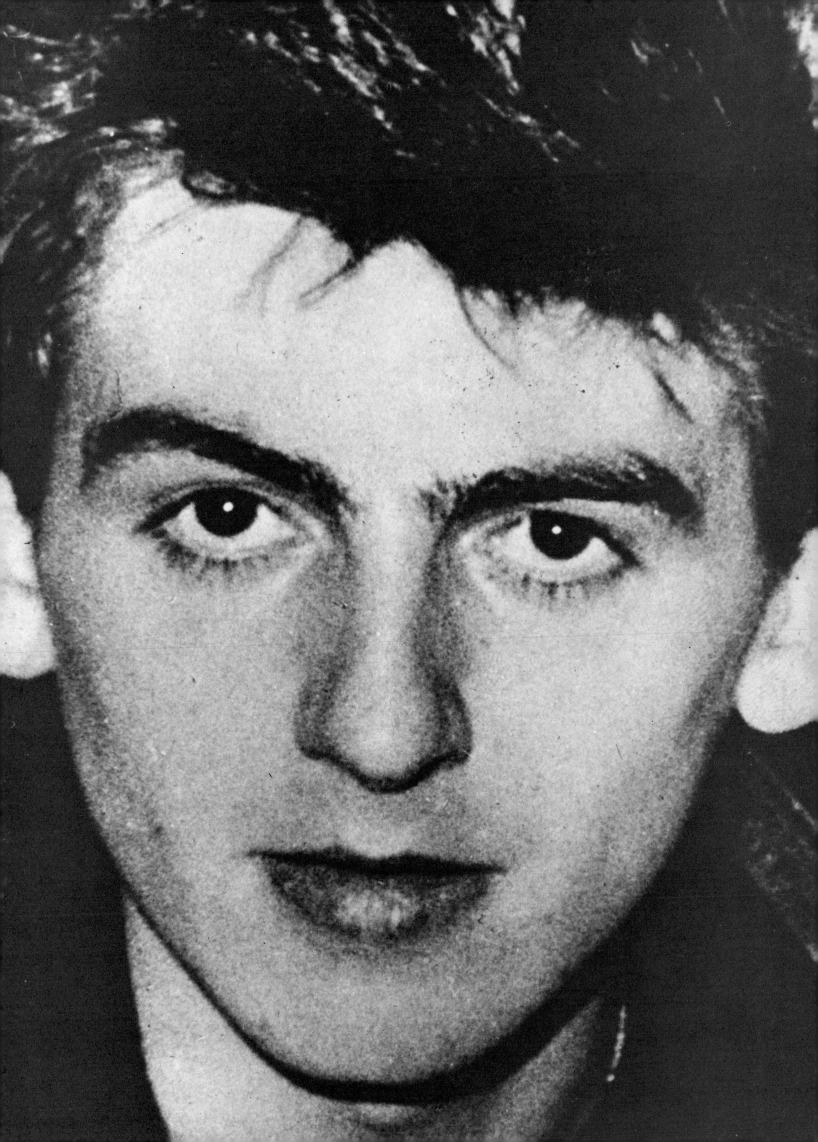

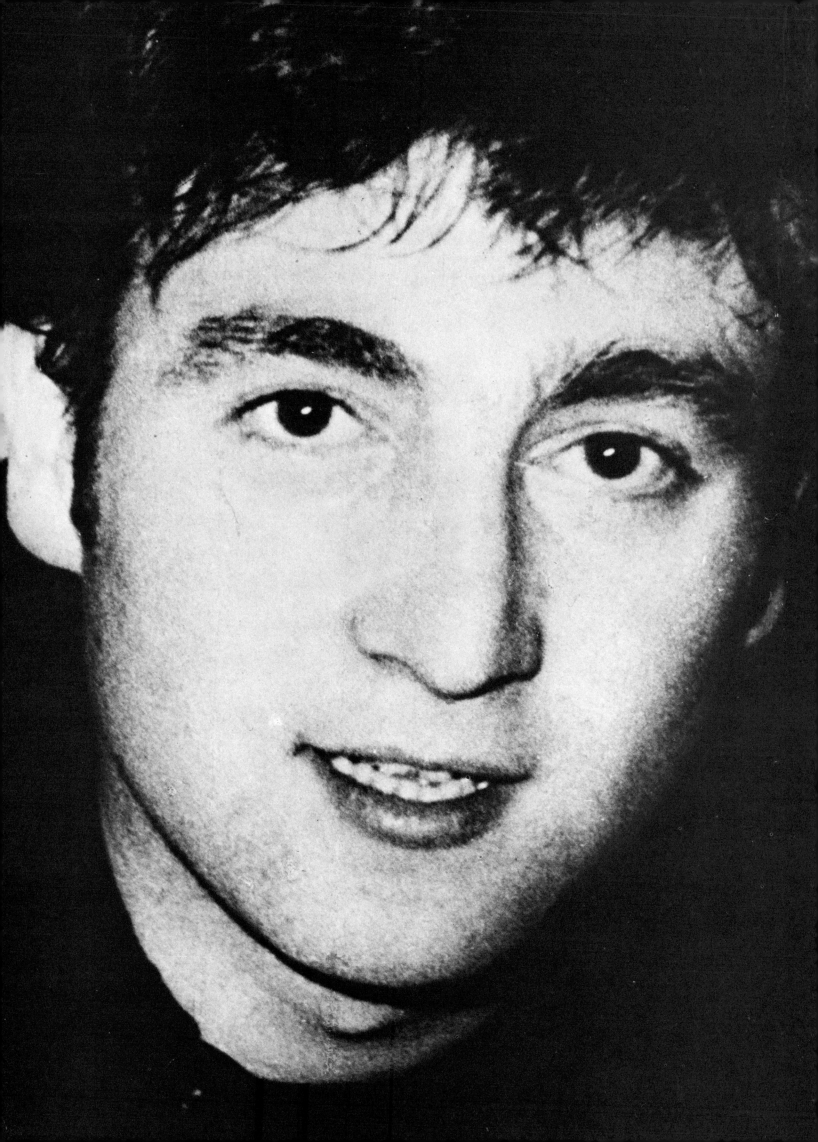

her two-week holiday visiting John, remembers the pills as "necessary," but has also described a typical night when John "fell about the stage in hysterical convulsions with so much booze and so many pills inside him that he was no way in control. . . . That night ended with John sitting on the edge of the stage in a very unsteady manner with an ancient wooden toilet seat round his neck, his guitar in one hand, and a bottle of beer in the other, completely out of his mind." After that, the boys went out to party.

Given the constant physical and chemical

Left: 1961, John. Top: George and John on Hamburg truck, with Stu in profile. Above: In the beginning, when the Beatles were going nowhere, John would shout, "Where are we going, fellas?" "To the top, Johnny!" they shouted back. "What top?" "To the Toppermost of the Poppermost, Johnny!" By 1962 the dream came true and they were voted the most popular group in Liverpool by readers of a local pop paper.

strain under which the band operated, it is no surprise that they often fought among themselves. Pete Best took the brunt of the abuse, but Paul was equally hard on Stuart. Though some of the tension was simply the result of different personalities grinding together under constant pressure, Cynthia observed that Paul "was fed up playing rhythm guitar along with John. He wanted desperately to expand his musical ability by playing left-hand bass, which of course would leave Stuart out in the cold." Whether he jumped or was pushed remains unclear, but Stuart—drawn both by Astrid and by a grant to study at Hamburg's Art College—remained behind when the group returned to Liverpool. He was to die of a brain hemorrhage less than a year later.

But before they left, Stuart indirectly gave them a most important parting gift: One day he abandoned his Teddy Boy look and let Astrid brush his hair forward into what she called "the French style." When he arrived at the Top Ten that night, he was ragged un-

Left: John, Paul and George on a Hamburg rooftop, in leather with cowboy overtones. Top: Before he joined the Beatles in 1962, Ringo played three years with Rory Storm (shown with Ringo) and the Hurricanes. Above: A group shot with Pete Best, third from left, 1961. Overleaf: 1961 portrait against the autographed walls of the Cavern Club. Note Gerry and the Pacemakers' signature behind Pete Best's head.

31

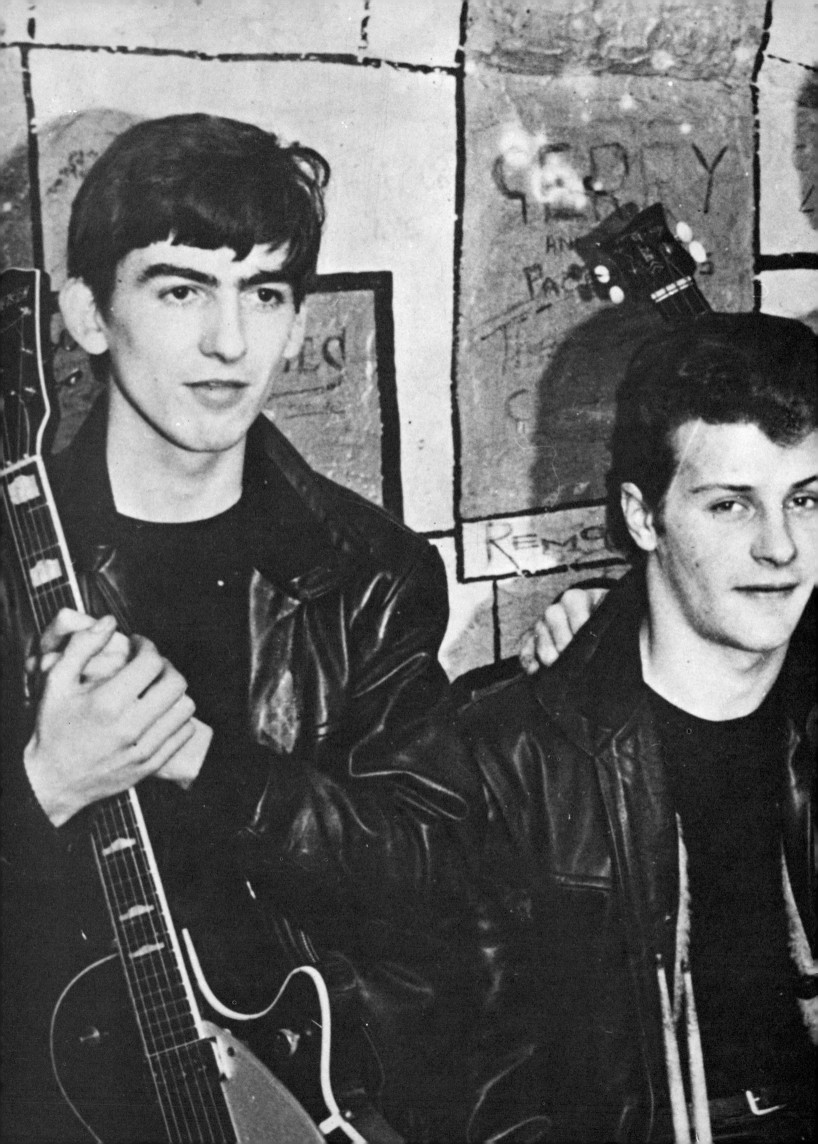

mercifully. But two days later, George followed suit. Then Paul, and finally John. The new look was the first of many that would mark the Beatles' progress from a local phenomenon to worldwide stars. Only Pete Best resisted it.

The received version of the event that would finally launch the Beatles begins with one Raymond Jones, a leather-jacketed Liverpool Ted who walked into Nems Music Store on an October afternoon in 1961 and asked for "My Bonnie," by a group called the Beatles. Nems was owned by 27-year-old Brian Epstein. His policy was that no Nems customer would go unsatisfied; when Brian tried to track the record down he discovered it was a German import. Other requests soon came in. Intrigued, Epstein researched further into the Beatles and learned —as he recalled in his autobiography, "what I hadn't known before"—that the Beatles weren't a German band at all, but a local group even then playing at the Cavern Club. He went to see them, and history was blah, blah, blah. . . .

This is a splendidly romantic, and probably apocryphal, story. By the time Epstein first saw the Beatles, he had been writing a column in Bill Harry's *Mersey Beat* music paper for more than three months. According to Harry, Epstein was an attentive reader,

Left: A bearded Ringo, 1961. Above: At the Cavern Club with Ringo, 1962. George's Mum remembered the club as a "real dump. The walls ran with sweat, shorting the amps, but the boys would just carry on all the same, singing on their own."

We were just in a daydream until Brian came along. We'd no idea what we were doing or where we'd agreed to be.

[JOHN]

and according to Epstein himself, he was a compulsively comprehensive record retailer. Thus it seems impossible that he would have missed *Mersey Beat*'s overly optimistic page-one headline, "BEATLES SIGN RECORDING CONTRACT!" It's true, however, that his first sight of the Beatles in performance was at the Cavern's lunchtime show on November 9th, 1961. He stayed with them for the rest of his life.

At twenty-seven, Epstein was a curious blend of failure and success. The eldest son of a successful furniture merchant, he was the first in his family to make the great leap upward to a British public school, Wrekin College. There, rather to his surprise, Epstein finished at the top of his class in art. And there, to his parents' amazement, he decided he wanted to become a dress designer. This notion was sharply rejected as "not manly," so he left Wrekin and entered the family business as a salesman.

But this skill didn't help when he was drafted into the army, nor in an eighteen-month stint studying theater at the Royal Academy of Dramatic Art. So in 1957 he

This first publicity shot of the Beatles shows manager Brian Epstein's strong influence. Memos typed on Brian's monogrammed stationery instructed them not to smoke, laugh, eat or talk while onstage.

abandoned art for commerce, and by 1961 had made Nems the North's most important record store. Though not associated with Liverpool's burgeoning beat clubs—he was too old and too proper—he was important enough that the Cavern audience gave him a round of applause when he was introduced after the Beatles' show.

Epstein, who thought the Beatles "not very tidy and not very clean," nevertheless admitted their "considerable magnetism." Though he hadn't thought about managing them, he had them come by his store for a chat.

His motives for arranging this talk were muddled, but he certainly could identify with the Beatles in ways that made their differences of income and dress irrelevant. Like them, he was an outsider, a Liverpudlian in a country where London had the "real" culture, and neither the crease in his expensive trousers nor the cultivated polish in his voice could alter that fact. Though the Beatles

Left: Everything has a price tag but Brian, who poses in a London department store. Above: The Beatles and producer George Martin were presented with a silver disc when 'Please Please Me' went to the top of the British charts and sold a quarter of a million records. From their distinctive haircuts to their pointed boots (right), the Beatles marked their generation.

were unaware of the subtle lines of discrimination hedging Brian in—to them, he was a pretty posh sort—he was painfully aware that he was trapped.

To begin with, he was a Jew (years later, when a friend suggested that he should receive an MBE along with the Beatles, he wryly asked, "Don't you remember my name?"), and no matter what he accomplished, the genuinely powerful would always regard him as a grubby little tradesman. Finally, he was a homosexual in a country where the closet doors were firmly, if politely, shut. But in the Beatles' raw energies he found more than sexual magnetism; he felt a force that could crack the barriers of class and caste. And that might at last let him escape his steadily less-challenging life as a Liverpool retailer.

The Beatles knew they needed a manager. They had fallen out with Allan Williams over his commission on their Top Ten Club contract, and though Pete Best tried to keep track of things, he was an inadequate substitute. Brian, in John's words, "looked effi-

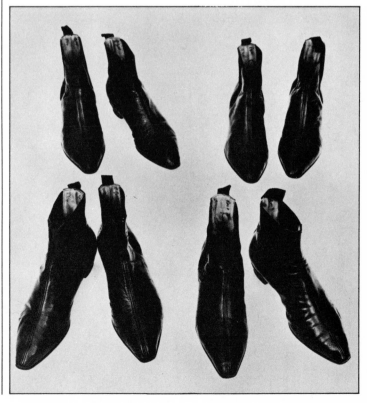

None of us had quite grasped what it was all about. It was washing over our heads like a huge tidal wave.

[RINGO]

cient and rich." Still, their first meeting was not a total success; Paul arrived an hour late. (He had, it seems, been taking a bath. When Epstein complained that Paul "would be *very* late," George responded, "And very clean.") After that initial experience, Brian decided he'd better check out the Beatles' reliability. Among those he contacted was Williams,

Reflections of Ringo and George before a concert. When a reporter asked what they called their hairstyle, George answered, "Arthur."

who told him, according to Epstein's autobiography, "Have nothing to do with them. They will let you down." Williams, characteristically, remembers his advice as less polite. "My honest opinion, Brian, is: Don't touch them with a fucking bargepole."

He did more than touch them; he remade them. Not their music—Epstein was smart enough to know where his expertise ended—but their image, their *personae*. In his autobiography, Epstein remembered arranging retail store windows with the note that he "was, and still am, mad about the way things should be displayed." And he brought to the Beatles precisely that veneer of juvenile class that one would expect from a provincial window dresser. Cute velvet suits replaced leather, ties adorned necks that once sported graying T-shirts, and the greasy hair grew fluffy and clean, clean, clean.

None of this was accomplished without strain. John contented himself with such minor acts of rebellion as loosening his tie during their shows (later complaining that Paul would make him straighten it). For Paul, the problem was different; the changes in their image were fine, but he felt the closeness of the Lennon-McCartney team threatened by the growing friendship between John and Brian. Indeed, once Paul refused to show up for a performance at the Birkenhead Technical College because when Brian called for him with the van, he had picked John up first.

At this time, there was a fair amount of Liverpool speculation about the precise nature of the relationship between Brian and his Beatles. The rumor that Pete and Brian were lovers died fairly quickly when Best left the group (and was interred when he married), but stories about John and Brian grew. They peaked when Brian took John to Spain with him for a vacation, and John apparently found them challenging enough to his macho image that he was still going out of his way to deny them in interviews years after the band had broken up. At the time, however, he defended his heterosexual virtue with more than words; during one Liverpool party, the Cavern's rotund emcee, Bob Wooler, unwisely suggested that Brian and John had a little something going. Flying into a fury,

---

Left: Candid shots of John, George, Ringo and Paul. Right: Said Ringo, "I didn't feel I really belonged until after the first two years. It was just them—the Beatles—and me, the new drummer."

On this next number those in the cheap seats please clap. The rest of you can rattle your jewelry.

[JOHN]

John knocked the older man down and repeatedly kicked him in the face. The scene was ugly enough that Brian had to go to Wooler's office the next day and make it up with him. Brian offered money, John offered an apology; Wooler accepted both.

But for all his active and indirect influence on the Beatles' image, Brian didn't change their music. The Beatles had early on discovered an aesthetic of noise. Paul remembers Hamburg: "We didn't worry about arrangements of anything. If we had trouble with the overworked amplifiers—we had to plug two guitars into one—I'd just chuck everything in and start leaping around the stage or rush to the piano and start playing some

Left: On stage and off the ground in 1963. Above: The Beatles are presented to Princess Margaret at the Royal Variety Show.

chords . . . it was noise and beat all the way.'' So they kept their hard, aggressive rock 'n' roll sound. The tapes of their 1962 performances at Hamburg's Star Club dispel forever the revisionist myth that the Beatles were society's safe alternative to the demonic Rolling Stones. In these performances—George's flailing guitar on "Roll Over Beethoven," John's explosive vocal on "Sweet Little Sixteen," and Paul's loonily energetic send-up of Little Richard's "Long Tall Sally"—the Beatles kick ass.

The phrase is not accidental; under Epstein's tutelage, the Beatles became a curious metaphor for his life. Though he played the exceedingly proper businessman by day, Epstein's nights were anything but staidly suburban. John has spoken of Epstein's "having hellish tempers and fits and lock-outs and y'know he'd vanish for days. . . . The whole business would fuckin' stop 'cause he'd be on sleeping pills for days on end and wouldn't wake up. Or he'd be missing, y'know, beaten up by some docker down the Old Kent Road." When Epstein went to London seeking a recording contract for the band, he was fully aware of the violent musical assault that lay just beneath their well-scrubbed surface; the born salesman sold not only the Beatles, but himself.

"It's security we got to wanting," Paul said, "and unless things really fold in, we'll have it. As I see it, we have a great opportunity to lead a fantastically lucky life." Above: Ringo and Paul on a rainy London street. Right: The silver Beatles go gold.

Small wonder that he succeeded. His charm was genuine, his power as the North's largest retailer considerable enough to guarantee him the chance to use it. Finally, of course, his product was genuinely special. He weathered some courteously deferential turn-downs, but by the end of July, George Martin had agreed to record them for Parlophone Records. They were on their way: John, Paul, George . . . and Pete.

They didn't tell Pete about the recording contract. They had been considering replacing him for a long time; now, on the eve of their recording contract, they wanted to do it at once. Though Epstein opposed any change, the dirty job of firing Pete fell to him. He did it with as much grace as possible, shifting some of the blame to George Martin, but the Liverpool uproar was immediate. Best was a particular local favorite—partly because he'd stuck with his Ted style, and partly because his mother unceasingly promoted him at her popular Casbah Club. Once *Mersey Beat* ran its exclusive "Beatles Change Drummer" story, all hell broke loose; an angry, chanting crowd of Best's fans gathered at the Cavern to protest Ringo's first appearance as a Beatle. Brian chose not to accompany the band, and prudently remained in his office, but George, with no such option, struggled to push his way to the stage. He got a black eye in the process.

In that summer of 1962, Ringo—born Richard Starkey—was at loose ends. Having pretty well split with Rory Storm and the Hurricanes, he was thinking seriously enough about emigration to write the Houston Chamber of Commerce enquiring about the work situation in Texas. At the age of twenty-two, he still wanted to be a cowboy.

Not that there was much else for him to do but dream. Ringo had been born into a tenement poverty that made even the Harrisons look genteel. Which was only the first of his problems. His parents were divorced when he was three years old, and he grew up in the Dingle, one of rough Liverpool's roughest sections, where his mother supported the family by working as a barmaid. And in addition to being grindingly poor, young Richard Starkey was sickly as well.

At six, he suffered a burst appendix and peritonitis, spent ten weeks in a coma and more than a year in the hospital. He returned to school a year behind in lessons, completely unable to read and write. Though a neighbor eventually helped him catch up, he never tried for an academic placement, but went to the local trade school instead.

I screamed the loudest when Paul and George shook their heads. I've never seen anything so fab in my life.

[A FAN]

At first his luck seemed to change. His mother remarried—easing the family's perpetually strapped finances—and he did moderately well in school. But at age thirteen, he contracted pleurisy and returned to the hospital. There he developed complications and was transferred to another institution where he spent almost two full years, leaving it at the age of fifteen. By then, with virtually no schooling, he had reached graduation age. Still sickly, he could do no physically demanding labor, but found a job as a messenger and eventually worked his way into an apprentice program as a fitter. That was when the skiffle craze hit.

His stepfather, pleased to see Ringo getting involved with anything, bought him a set of used drums. Within a year, with help from his paternal grandfather, he acquired a better set. Since drums were expensive, he was—perhaps for the first time in his life—in demand.

He sat in with several local groups, but his real break came in 1959, when Rory Storm was offered a summer's engagement at Butlin's, a working-class resort. Storm asked

Holding back the Beatle fans. Parliament debated the wisdom of using British police for "extra and dangerous duty" to protect the Beatles. One MP suggested that the police should withdraw and see what happened. His suggestion was ignored.

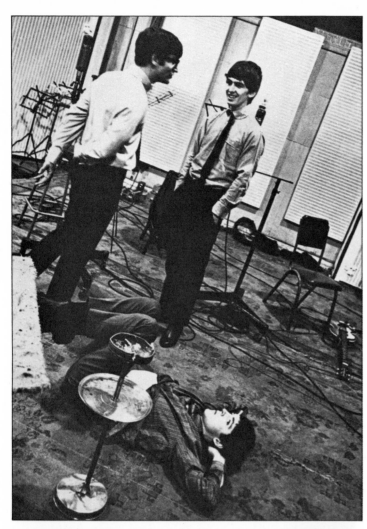

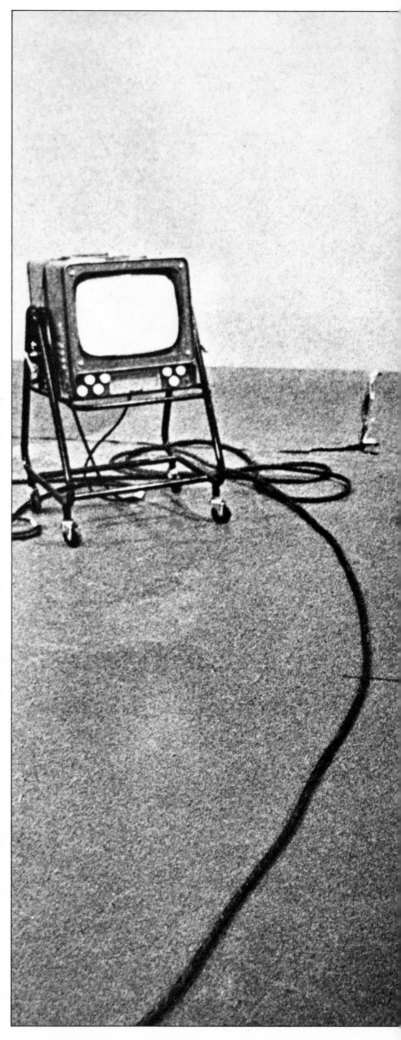

Ringo to join the band full-time, and after discovering that he could earn three times his apprentice wage, Ringo signed on. Somewhat scrawny—and, let's face it, funny looking—Ringo was an immediately recognizable figure on stage; he became so popular that his twenty-first birthday party drew the cream of Liverpool's beat groups to his family's house. The Beatles, back in Hamburg on their second trip, didn't come.

The Beatles in a London recording studio. When asked how they decide who sings the lead, John replied, "We just get together and whoever knows most of the words sings the lead."

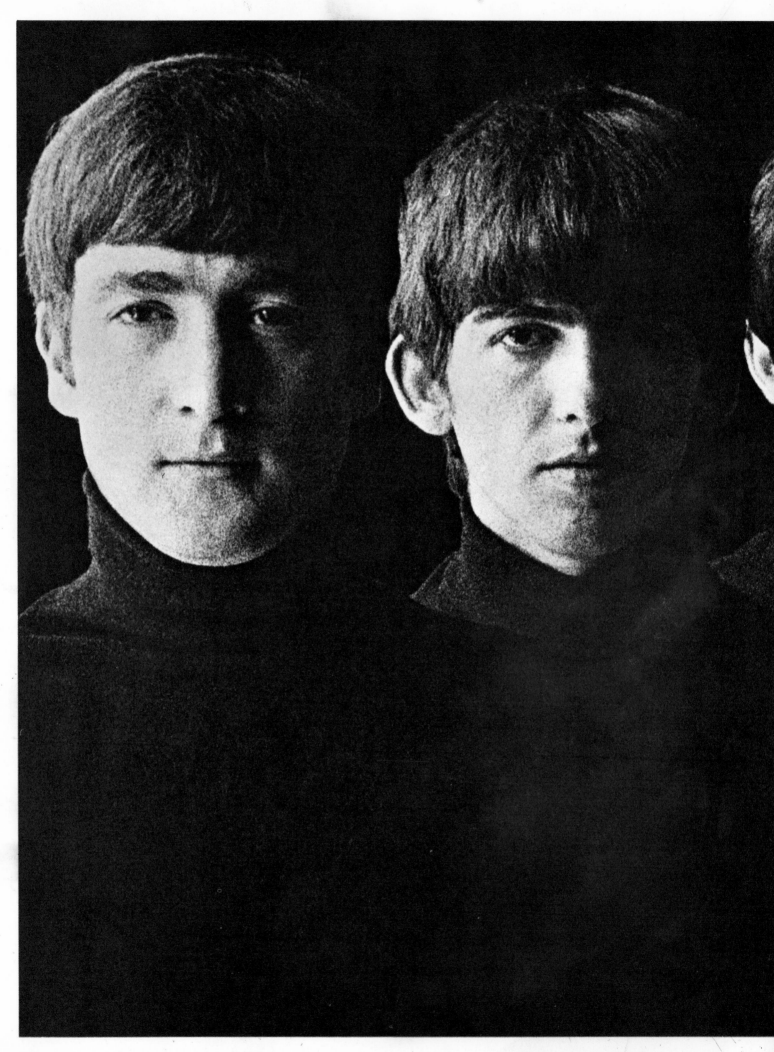

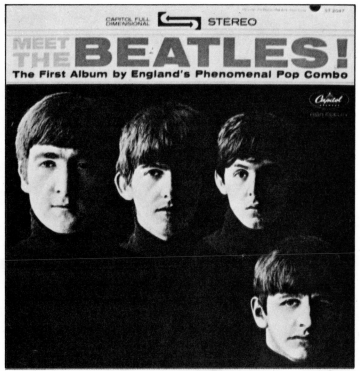

The thing is, we're all really the same person. We're just four parts of the one.

[PAUL]

Ringo eventually met the Beatles when he went with Rory Storm to Hamburg, where he often sat in with them (including those legendary sessions recorded at the Star Club). When Storm's booking was over, Ringo liked Hamburg enough to stay on to back Tony Sheridan. But after a while, he too returned to England. He was balancing the attractions of Texas against those of another summer's steady work behind Storm when John called, asking him to become a Beatle.

He would, said John, have to brush his hair forward—something Best had staunchly

Robert Freeman's photograph of the four faces, half lit, graced the cover of the first LP that launched them worldwide. It was called 'With the Beatles' in England and 'Meet the Beatles' in America.

refused to do—but could keep his sideburns. He would earn £25 a week. The going rate for Liverpool bands was only £20, so Ringo agreed. When the Beatles went down to London in September to make their first record, Ringo went with them.

Assessing his skills years after fame had struck, Ringo says he was only "one of the two best drummers in Liverpool" at that time. In other words, his playing was powerful but crude, designed as much to move a crowded dance floor as to drive a band. His sound was, and pretty much remained, all cymbals and toms; the drum roll and, despite the occasional rim shot, the snare were for sissies.

New to the band, he was especially awkward in the studio. Though recording was much, much simpler in the days before multi-tracking and million-dollar production jobs, Ringo's sound seemed too raw for records. So producer George Martin arranged to have session musician Andy White play drums with the band, leaving Ringo with the ma-

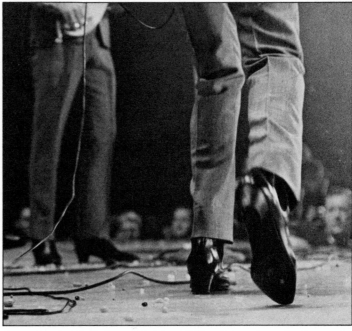

Left: London Palladium, October 1963. Above: Stage-level view of essential Beatle elements—guitar leads, jelly beans and Cuban-heeled boots. Overleaf: On the Champs-Elysées. The Beatles played the Paris Olympia for three weeks in January 1964.

racas on "P.S. I Love You" and the tambourine on "Love Me Do." Whether or not Martin was right is an interesting question: Ringo's drumming did appear on the British album version of "Love Me Do," and the difference between his approach and White's makes it clear that as Epstein softened their image, so Martin conventionalized their sound.

But the fact of the record—their record, at last—mattered more to the boys than did Ringo's temporary embarrassment. Fired with enthusiasm, they went back on the ballroom circuit. Ringo's deadpan charm soon exorcised Best's ghost, and it seemed the lucky four had nothing to do but wait for stardom.

It didn't come quite as magically as they'd wished. Though spurred by sales in the North (where Epstein's firm ordered it heavily), their record made only a small dent on the British charts. By the time it peaked at number seventeen and began its fall, they were back to club drudgery in Hamburg. But they had already recorded their second single, and when "Please Please Me" was released in January 1963, it took only a month to become Britain's number one hit. With it,

Above: When 'I Want to Hold Your Hand' went to No. 1 on the U.S. charts, Brian (sporting a chamber pot) celebrated with George Martin and the world's now-famous foursome. Above right: Arriving in Paris, Ringo renames British European Airways.

the Beatles were on their way.

Not, mind you, that anyone outside of the music business paid much attention. Though Maureen Cleave of the *London Evening Standard* did a feature on them, stressing their quaint Liverpoolness, that was about the extent of press interest. But in May, risking hubris, Epstein hired the Beatles their own full-time press agent. Number one was nice and more than the band had dared dream when they were backing strippers in a Liverpool basement, but Epstein had a larger vision. Though the word didn't yet exist, he was already inventing "Beatlemania."

In America, records even now "break" (make their move up the sales charts) primarily through radio play. People hear the song and *then* buy it. They have this opportunity (or, as some would have it, are trapped by this manipulation) because even the smallest hamlet has one or two radio stations pumping out "Top Forty" pop. That was certainly not the case in 1963 England. Though Radio Luxembourg beamed its powerful pop wattage across the British Isles, the dominant BBC sound was then very much "Auntie Beeb." No rude noises need apply.

So British groups toured intensively, angled for the rare television appearance and courted the press—both the innumerable pop weeklies and the general papers. At this point in their careers, only the music weeklies showed much interest in the Beatles; despite occasional prodding and a continual stream of "exclusives" distributed by their publicist, only one article about the band appeared in a national paper during the first half of 1963.

But they worked hard as opening acts for the likes of Helen Shapiro and Tommy Roe and finally co-headlined with Roy Orbison. Their third record, "From Me to You," was released during this period, and it too became a number-one hit, boosted by their first national TV appearance. They began to draw crowds—and jellybeans, which George incautiously had mentioned liking to a music paper.

They also drew a lot of cripples, a curiosity they still haven't quite figured out, though it seems to have had something to do with the clean, cheery image they were projecting under Brian's tutelage. Their long-time road manager, Neil Aspinall, who had been with them even in pre-Ringo days, recalled, "We always got masses of cripples. They would be in the dressing room when we arrived at the theater. The management would let them in, thinking we'd love to see them, as we were supposed to be such lovely blokes." It is not recorded that they performed any miraculous cures during this period.

Despite their growing army of fans, crippled and otherwise, the Beatles were still a Liverpool group. Though in August, they released "She Loves You," which made its

predictable climb to number one, their major national breakthrough came with their October 13th appearance on the BBC's live variety show, *Sunday Night at the London Palladium*. Though the show's home audience was estimated at about fifteen million people, it was the London fans who finally made the Beatles front-page news.

Fans had been turned away from sold-out Beatles shows almost routinely for the previous seven months, but it had never happened in London before. As the crowd gathered, journalists and television crews arrived to report on it. Other teenagers, hearing the stories, came down to see what the action was. Which brought still more reporters and

At first Paris was cold to the Beatles. A reporter asked John, "The French have not made up their minds about the Beatles; what do you think of them?" "Oh, we like the Beatles," he replied, "they're gear." Before long, Paris shops were selling Beatle wigs.

a thoroughly bewildered police force. The police, attempting to be helpful, moved the getaway car to what they thought was a more advantageous position. Unfortunately, they neglected to inform the Beatles of this change, and the four had to run a desperate fifty-yard gauntlet through a swirling mob of fans whose hysteria had been steadily rising during the long wait. This photogenic dash was news.

More important, it was the sort of determinedly unserious news for which the English press and public—battered by the unfolding scandals of the gradually less amusing Profumo-Keeler affair—were subconsciously eager. Instead of the Beatles story dying out when the group left London and went on tour, it grew—the media and the fans fed on one another as they had outside the Palladium. The datelines changed—Carlisle, Birmingham, Dublin (where the chief of police offered the wonderful observation that things were "all right until the mania degenerated into barbarism")—but the story was the same: Beatlemania.

The Beatles hardly noticed. The crowds looked the same to them as they had before the Palladium show; only the reporters were different, but you couldn't see them from the stage. Blissfully unaware of the effects of Heisenberg's Principle of Uncertainty, they set off on a brief Swedish tour. It was only when they returned to find their first screaming mob waiting for them at the airport that the enormity of their success began to sink in.

The seal was set on Beatlemania when the band was invited to play at the 1963 *Royal Variety Show*. They came to this event, which also included Sophie Tucker, Marlene Dietrich and Maurice Chevalier, less as subjects of the Queen than as visiting potentates. Asked by reporters if he thought the Beatles were being disloyal to their Liverpool fans by appearing in such fancy company, Ringo remarked only that he thought it would be nice to play drums for the Queen Mother.

Later on in November, they released their second British album, *With the Beatles*; it of course climbed rapidly up the charts, but the media focus stayed less on their music than on their Beatleness. It began to shift, however, from news stories about riots to sober analyses of precisely What This All Meant. As they had in Hamburg, the Beatles began to broaden their base of typical "fans" and

The low bows that Brian recommended became a Beatle trademark. Left and right: The Olympia Theater in Paris. "Mersey beaucoup," John said, acknowledging the audience's applause.

to capture the intelligentsia. Perhaps their crowning achievement, and the source of much private amusement, came when the *London Times* music critic offered a year-end appraisal opining that, " 'That Boy,' which figures prominently in Beatle programmes, is expressively unusual for its lugubrious music, but harmonically it is one of their most intriguing, with its chains of pandiatonic clusters, and the sentiment is acceptable because voiced cleanly and crisply. But harmonic interest is typical of their quicker songs too, and one gets the impression that they think simultaneously of harmony and melody, so firmly are the major tonic sevenths and ninths built into their tunes, and the flat submediant key switches, so natural in the Aeolian cadence at the end of 'Not a Second Time' (the chord progression that ends Mahler's *Song of the Earth*)." □

"Spending time with the Beatles," said one London reporter, is "like living it up with the Marx Brothers." Above: The Fab Four cavorting for the camera. Following pages: 1964, Paul, John, George and Ringo

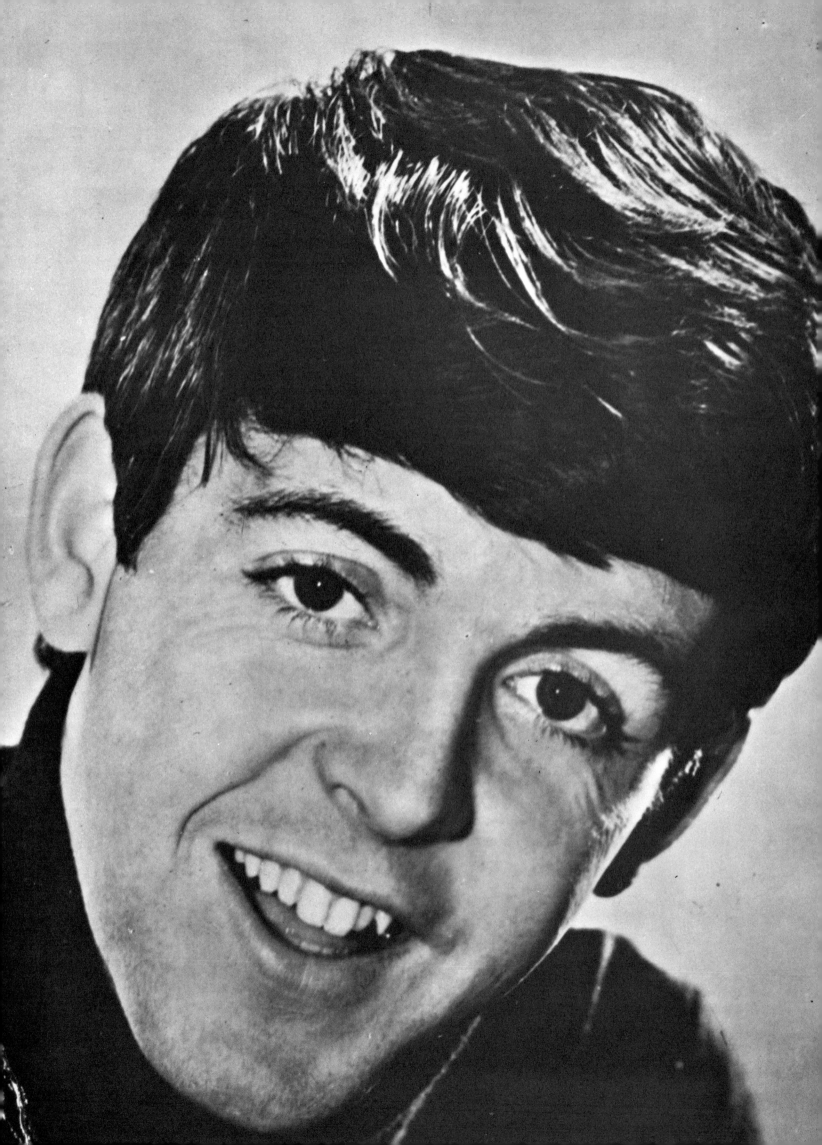

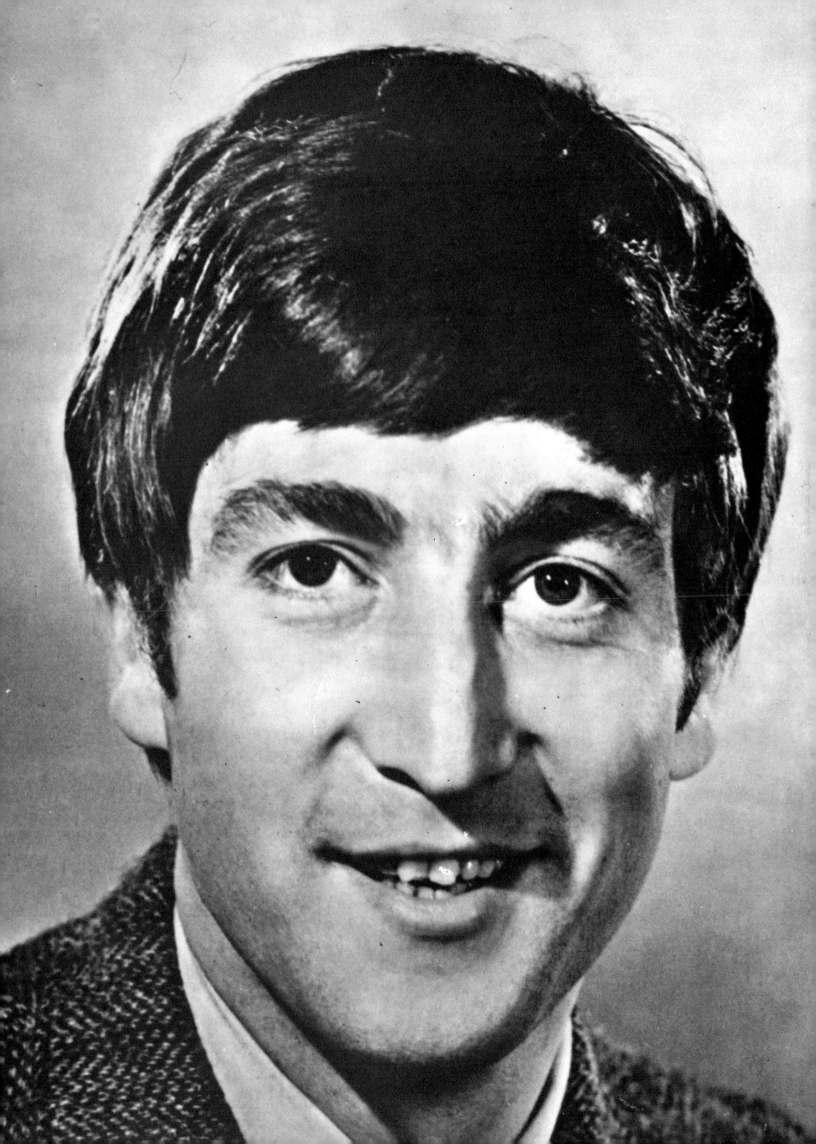

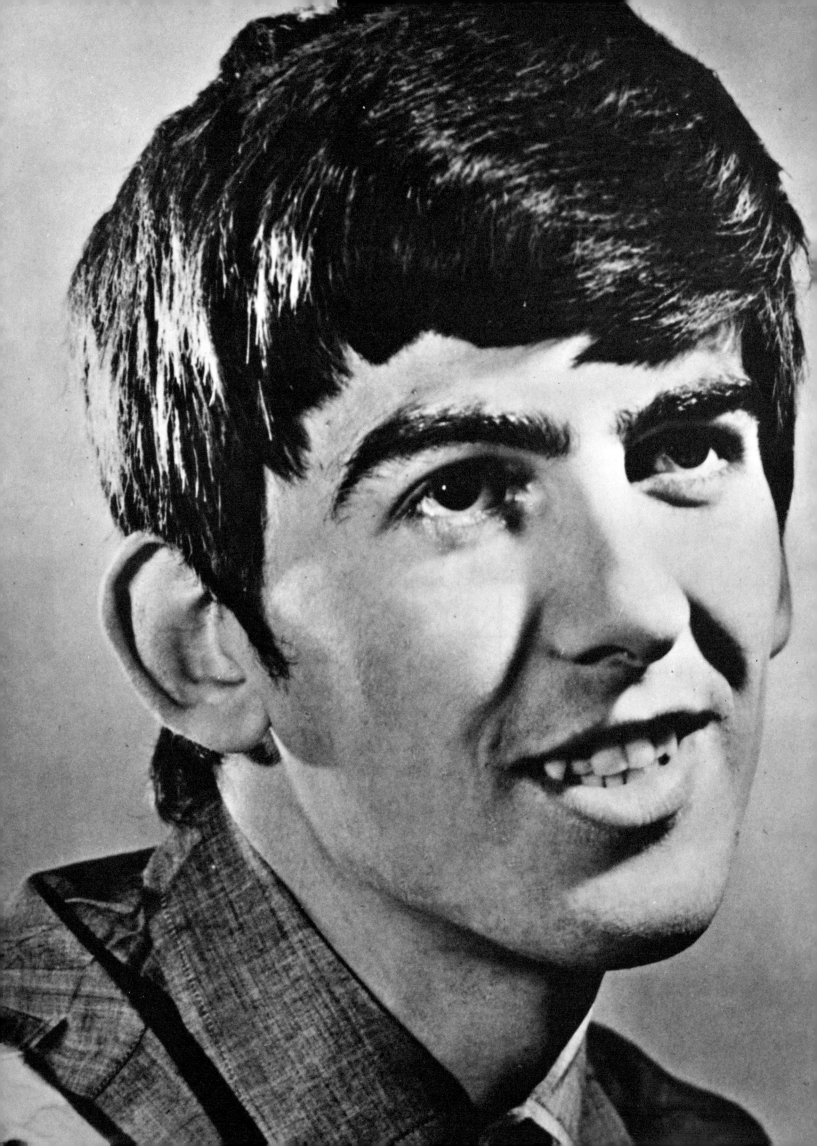

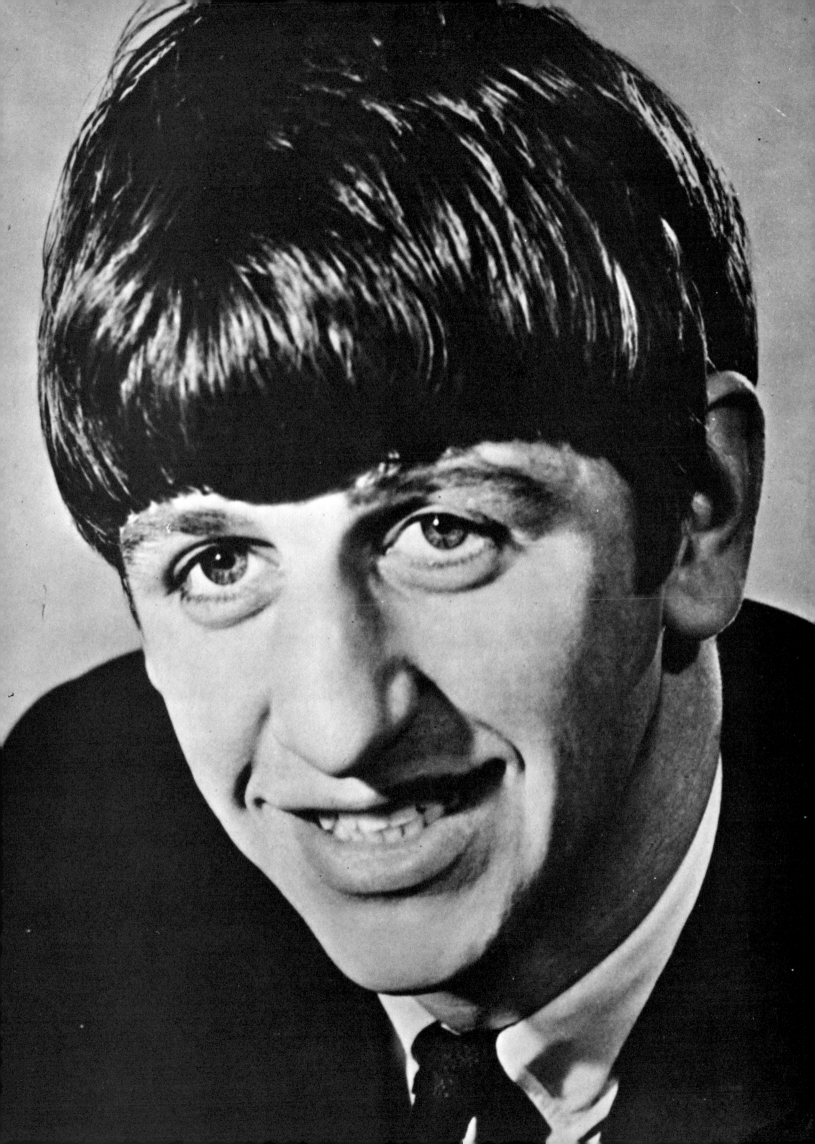

The Beatles Invade, Complete With Long Hair and Screaming Fans

Associated Press

Police strain to restrain the hundreds of Beatle fans as the British rock 'n' roll entourage rolls up to the Plaza Hotel

3,000 FANS GREET BRITISH BEATLES

4 Rock 'n' Roll Performers Hailed by Teen-Agers

By PAUL GARDNER

Multiply Elvis Presley by four, subtract six years from his age, add British accents and a sharp sense of humor. The answer: It's the Beatles (Yeah, Yeah, Yeah).

The rock 'n' roll group, which may become Britain's most successful export since the bowler, arrived at Kennedy International Airport yesterday and more than 3,000 teen-agers stood four deep on the upper arcade at the International Arrivals Building to greet them.

Disk jockeys who have an interest in Beatle records had urged the young people to welcome them. The quartet has sold 6 million records and earns as much as $10,000 a week for appearances. Five organizations, represented by at least 17 press agents, will share in the Beatles's American booty.

Official Impressed

An official at Kennedy Airport shook his head and said, "We've never seen anything like this here before. Never. Not even for kings and queens."

There were girls, girls and more girls. Whistling girls. Screaming girls. Singing girls. They held "Beatles, we love you" and "WELCOME" signs. When the Beatles's plane touched down at 1:20 P.M. the girls chanted, "We want Beatles."

The Beatles are Paul McCartney, 21 years old; Ringo Starr, 23; George Harrison, 21; and John Lennon, 23. They arrived by jet with their personal manager, one Beatle wife (Mrs. Lennon), two road managers and one press agent.

The Beatles will make their first live television appearance here Sunday evening on the Ed Sullivan show. On Tuesday, they will go to Washington for a concert at the Coliseum. On Wednesday, Lincoln's Birthday, they will give two shows at Carnegie Hall.

Next Sunday the Beatles will accompany Mr. Sullivan to Miami Beach for a performance in the Deauville Hotel. Their third TV appearance, which will be on tape, will be recorded here this weekend. They will return to London on Feb. 17.

The Beatles, who popularized rock 'n' roll in Britain, have added new gimmicks: tight pants, boots, and hair that never seems to be cut.

Danielle Landau, a 15-year-old from Brooklyn, oohed and aahed as the Beatles left the terminal. "They're different." she sighed, "They're just so different. I mean, all that hair. American singers are soooo clean-cut."

The Beatles are staying at the Plaza Hotel. They have a 10-room suite and a guard who is on duty 24 hours. They were driven into the city by four limousines—each Beatle had his own Cadillac.

Besides the screaming teen-agers, the Beatles were met by 200 reporters and photographers from newspapers, magazines, foreign publications, radio and television stations and teen-age fan magazir press conference was

While the Beat
ly on a plat'

New York Herald Tribune

Beatles! More Than Just a Word to the Wild

By Tom Wolfe
Of The Herald Tribune Staff

By 6:30 a. m. yesterday, half the kids from South Orange, N. J., to Seaford, L. I., were already up with their transistors plugged in their skulls. It was like a Civil Defense network or something. You could turn anywhere on the dial, WMCA, WCBS, WINS, almost any place, and get the bulletins: "It's B-Day! 6:30 a. m.! The Beatles left London 30 minutes ago! They're 30 minutes out over the Atlantic Ocean! Heading for New York!"

By I p. m., about 4,000 kids had finessed school and come skipping and screaming into the international terminal at Kennedy Airport. It took 110 police to herd them. At 1:20 p. m., the Beatles' jet arrived from London.

The Beatles left the plane and headed for customs inspection and everybody got their first live look at the Beatles' hair style, which is a mop effect that covers the forehead, some of the ears and most of the back of the neck. To get a better look, the kids came plunging down the observation deck, and some of them already had their combs out, raking their hair down over their foreheads as they ran.

Then they were crowding around the plate-glass windows overlooking the customs section, stomping on the floor in unison, some of them beating time by bouncing off the windows.

The Beatles—George Harrison, 20; John Lennon, 23; Ringo Starr, 23, and Paul McCartney, 21—are all short, slight kids from Liverpool who wear four-button coats, stovepipe pants, ankle-high black boots with Cuban heels. And droll looks on their faces. Their name is a play on the word "beat."

They went into a small room for a press conference,

while some of the girls tried to throw themselves over a retaining wall.

Somebody motioned to the screaming crowds outside. "Aren't you embarrassed by all this lunacy?"

"No," said John Lennon, "it's crazy."

"What do you think of Beethoven?"

"He's crazy," said Lennon. "Especially the poems. Lovely writer."

In the two years in which they have risen from a Liverpool rock-and-roll dive group to the hottest performers in the record business, they had seen much of this wildness before. What really got them were the American teenage car sorties.

The Beatles left the airport in four Cadillac limousines, one Beatle to a limousine, heading for the Plaza Hotel in Manhattan. The first sortie came almost immediately. Five kids in a powder blue Ford overtook the caravan on the expressway, and as they passed each Beatle, one guy hung out the back window and waved a red blanket.

A white convertible came up second, with the word BEETLES scratched on both sides in the dust. A police car was close behind that one with the siren going and the alarm light rolling, but the kids, a girl at the wheel and two guys in the back seat, waved at each Beatle before pulling over to exit with the cops gesturing at them.

In the second limousine, Brian Sommerville, the Beatles' press agent, said to one of the Beatles, George Harrison: "Did you see that, George?"

Harrison looked at the convertible with its emblem in the dust and said, "They misspelled Beatles."

But the third sortie succeeded all the way. A good-looking brunette. who said her name was Caroline Reynolds, of New Canaan, Conn., and Wellesley College, had paid a cab driver $10 to follow the caravan all the way into town. She cruised by each Beatle, smiling faintly,

and finally caught up with George Harrison's limousine at a light at Third Avenue and 63d St.

"How does one go about meeting a Beatle?" she said out the window.

"One says hello," Harrison said out the window.

"Hello!" she said. "Eight more will be down from Wellesley." Then the light changed and the caravan was off again.

At the Plaza Hotel, there were police everywhere. The Plaza, on Central Park South just off Fifth Ave., is one of the most sedate hotels in New York. The Plaza was petrified. The Plaza accepted the Beatles' reservations months ago, before knowing it was a rock-and-roll group that attracts teenage riots.

About 500 teen-agers, most of them girls, had shown up at the Plaza. The police had herded most of them behind barricades in the square between the hotel and the avenue. Every entrance to the hotel was guarded. The screams started as soon as the first limousine came into view.

The Beatles jumped out fast at the Fifth Avenue entrance. The teen-agers had all been kept at bay. Old ladies ran up and touched the Beatles on their arms and backs as they ran up the stairs.

After they got to the Plaza the Beatles rested up for a round of television appearances (the Ed Sullivan show Sunday), recordings (Capitol Records), concerts (Carnegie Hall, Wednesday) and a tour (Washington, Miami). The kids were still hanging around the Plaza hours after they went inside.

One group of girls asked everybody who came out, "Did you see the Beatles? Did you touch them?"

A policeman came up, and one of them yelled, "He touched a Beatle! I saw him!"

The girls jumped on the cops' arms and back, but it wasn't a mob assault. There were goony smiles all over their faces.

They are
Ringo Sta

Herald Tribune photo by IRA ROSENBERG

A BIT OF ALL RIGHT—The Beatles getting their first look, and hearing their first sounds in New York after flying in from London. From left are Ringo Starr, Paul McCartney, John Lennon and George Harrison, at bottom.

So this is America.They all seem out of their minds.

[RINGO]

"Operation USA," as Epstein modestly called it, began shortly after the *Royal Variety Show* in 1963, when he traveled to New York and took an impressive suite at the Regency Hotel. This foray, made at a time when the Beatles were still fulfilling dates at £50 and £60 a night, cost him over £2000. It was a huge gamble. Before the Beatles, rock 'n' roll traffic had all been one way; Little Richard was a hero in England, Cliff Richard an unknown in America. But Epstein didn't just manage the Beatles, he loved them. And he firmly believed he could buck the transatlantic trend. He was, however, the only one.

Airport arrivals and departures, jammed by shrieking fans and frazzled cops, were an evermore familiar Beatles event. Right: Heathrow, departing for America. Above: At the airport press conference one reporter asked, "Are you part of a social rebellion against the older generation?" "It's a dirty lie," said John.

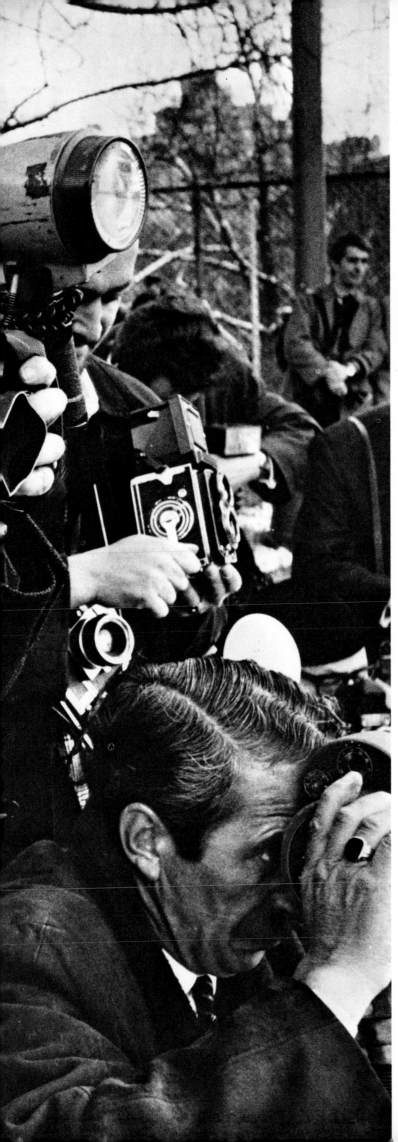

Capitol Records thought he was crazy. As an EMI subsidiary, that company had the American rights to the Beatles' records. But after a cursory listen to "Please Please Me" and "From Me to You," Capitol decided not to bother with them. Thus the singles were released into obscurity by Vee Jay Records, and even Vee Jay gave up on the third; "She Loves You" came out on the moribund Swan label. Since none of the three even cracked the Top 100, it was hard to argue with Capitol's decision.

Epstein did argue, of course, and spurred by conversations with the parent corporation in England, Capitol decided to release "I Want to Hold Your Hand." (Epstein later claimed he was sure the record would be a hit, but he nonetheless spent time shoring up his relations with Vee Jay as well.) His most visible arrangement, however, was with Ed Sullivan.

Despite its host's wooden on-camera style, the *Ed Sullivan Show* had the power to launch and crown careers; on a typical night, it drew five times as many viewers as the BBC's most popular program. It was always a conspicu-

Left: Photographers cover the Beatles in Central Park. Above: Ringo covers the photographers. Overleaf: Fans in extremis outside the Plaza

We can stand each other better now than when we first met.
[GEORGE]

ously international program (mimics gleefully parodied such pseudo-Sullivan specialties as "914 Polish dentists dancing and drilling for your delight"), and Sullivan's scouts regularly scoured European circuses for performers who might make it on American TV. Even if the Beatles had been nothing more than quaint novelties, they would have been a natural for him.

But he felt they were more than that. He had been at London Airport when mobs stormed the Beatles on their return from Stockholm and had no doubt at all what he was seeing. "I made up my mind that this was the same sort of mass hit hysteria that had characterized the Elvis Presley days," he told *The New York Times*. Elvis' career exploded after Sullivan had given him an unprecedented three-time spot on his show—albeit only from the waist up. His reporter's instincts quivering, Sullivan knew the Beatles

were "really big"; he wanted them, live and exclusive, on his show.

Epstein was, of course, inclined to agree. As a result, he didn't seek top money (indeed, the Beatles received $2400 per show, less than half of Sullivan's going rate), but top billing—three weeks in a row.

After two days of intensive negotiations, they agreed on a contract. One might imagine that Epstein would then have relaxed and waited for television to work its magic. But no. He had seen the Beatles bend the barriers of class and age in England, and he believed that they might well do the same thing in America. Yet Epstein knew that the radio-influenced mass market was too big a job for even the most energetic salesman, so he used his fluent, proper-British charm to woo the American press. Through him, the Beatles became the first pop act to get their break by means of the print medium.

And in a pretty classy way, too. The first significant Beatles stories on this side of the Atlantic ran in *The New Yorker* and *The New York Times Magazine*. The *Times* piece was essentially a news story—a datelined piece on Beatlemania that had been written with extensive assistance from the Beatles' British

Left: The flu kept George in bed at the Plaza during rehearsals. Right: When Sullivan first met them he thought it would be ridiculous to give a British group top billing when one had never made it in the States. Overleaf: George once said, "The nicest thing is to open up the newspapers and not find yourself in them."

New York World-Tele
The Sun
How Castro Plot
Fishermen Sent to Tri
Ex-Envoy Charges
Gag on Panama
In Ho
Advisers to Rockefe
Too Many for Com

press office—but *The New Yorker* was Epstein on his own. Both the interview and the journal he chose for it made Epstein's remarkable strategy clear. To capture England, the Beatles had first captured its kids (and that after a lengthy grind in bars and dance halls) but they were going to gobble down all America in a single gulp.

Capitol Records, which had been partially roused from its slumber by the news that Brian had lined up the Ed Sullivan shows, came fully awake with the January 13th, 1964, release of the Beatles' fourth single. When "I Want to Hold Your Hand" cracked the charts and went to number one, the record company began investing in the Beatles' future. During the three weeks before the band arrived in America, Capitol spent the then-unprecedented sum of $50,000 promoting them. Working with Brian, they hired sixteen press agents to whip up interest in the Beatles' impending arrival. As if by magic, stickers reading THE BEATLES ARE COMING

The 'Ed Sullivan Show' had 50,000 requests for the 728 available seats, and 73,000 viewers tuned in to watch the Beatles. Elvis sent a congratulatory telegram. Following pages: The CBS marquee (left) and the performance live and on TV

Which is the bigger threat to your careers... the H-bomb or dandruff? The H-bomb. We've already got dandruff.

[RINGO]

began to show up all over major cities, and important disc jockeys received not only the usual press kit, but Beatle wigs and a special record that allowed them to conduct "interviews" and receive the answers in the boys' own Liverpool voices. All over the country, radio stations struggled to see which could identify itself most closely with the Fab Four; in New York, where competition for advertising dollars was most intense, the Top Forty stations broadcast virtually minute-by-minute bulletins tracking the Beatles' airborne progress across the Atlantic.

The flight itself was a hubbub of activity

—a microcosm of the scene that would greet the Beatles when they landed. In addition to the squads of British reporters accompanying the tour at their papers' expense (the birth of the rock 'n' roll junket came after the Beatles' success mushroomed record-company receipts), a number of quick-thinking American businessmen had also booked seats. Smelling money, they literally could not wait for the Beatles to get to America. Brian, who was already in the process of setting up an American-based company to license the Beatles' name for various products, met with them in relays. His concern, he said, was that the Beatles' names and pictures be associated only with "quality products," and he turned down those that didn't fit the image he wanted the band to project. Among the offers he felt obliged to decline was one that would have resulted in an "official Beatles" sanitary napkin.

It seemed that virtually everything else was approved, however, and the Beatles' progress was heralded by such dubious devices as official Beatles lunchboxes, T-shirts, pajamas, pants, sweatshirts, three-button tennis shirts, and—of course—wigs. (These last were manufactured by the Lowell Toy Corporation, which pumped out more than 15,000 a day.)

In spite of all this, the boys themselves were nervous, and in the plane on the way over, Paul turned to Phil Spector—the American producer whose presence was a symbol that they were arriving in more ways than one —and asked: "Since America has always had everything, why should we be over there

By now Beatle wigs were everywhere and even John Paul Getty (left) succumbed to the fashion. But real Beatle hair was in even more demand. A reporter grabs a handful (right), to Ringo's dismay. Following pages: Photos from the Beatles' three-day stay in New York—a visit to Central Park, rehearsal for the 'Ed Sullivan Show' and jelly bean madness

Someone asked me why I wore rings on my fingers and I told him it's because I can't fit them through my nose.

[RINGO]

making money? They've got their own groups. What are we going to give them that they don't already have?"

Though he needn't have worried—nobody anywhere had the Beatles—Paul's question

At Miami Beach, Florida. When asked the reason they were the most popular singing group, John answered, "We've no idea. If we did, we'd get four long-haired boys and become their managers." Following pages: The Beatles approach the stage and the shrieks commence, then back to the Florida sun.

94

was reasonable. They might turn out to be, as Sullivan had intuited, another Elvis—an imported variation on the generation-defining theme. But that sort of success seemed almost too easy. Fueled by the New York radio stations' genial conspiracy, more than 4000 screaming teenagers waited to greet the Beatles as they left their plane. In addition to the regular complement of airport police, one hundred and ten of New York's Finest

---

When I feel my head start to swell, I just look at Ringo and know we're not supermen.

[JOHN]

were required to hold back the mob's frenzied charges. "We've never seen anything like this here before," panted one airport official, "never." He was perhaps too harried to comment on the crowd's most surprising feature: A number of its young men were already wearing their hair brushed forward.

Years later, long hair would become unremarkable even in the nation's boardrooms, but in 1963, it was news. Indeed, most of the

skeptical crowd of New York reporters rounded up by Epstein's press agents imagined that hair length would be the only news. Popular singers were hardly regarded as founts of wisdom—or even of coherence. On those rare occasions when Colonel Tom Parker had let reporters talk to America's greatest pop star, Elvis had seldom come up with anything more quotable than "Yessir" and "No, ma'am."

But Brian believed that the Beatles could charm adult America. And why not? If the Queen Mother had thought they were cute, so should the United States. Amid the popping of flashbulbs in the airport terminal, they brought to their first American press conference a mixture of sass and cynicism that established them as the reporters' intellectual peers. And in some cases, their superiors.

This was even bigger news than long hair. It was also a Trojan Horse, for even while the Beatles' wit made adults breathe easier, their sass allied them to the young. It was Epstein's promotional genius that had gotten the reporters to the airport in the first place, but it was the Beatles themselves who rewarded his faith by ad libbing their way through a press conference whose exchanges passed virtually overnight into folklore.

Will you sing for us?
John: We need money first.

How do you account for your success?
John: We have a press agent.

You mention Beethoven in one of your songs. What do you think of him?

The Beatles met Cassius Clay in Miami just three days before he became World Heavyweight Champion and changed his name to Muhammad Ali. Clay said he was the greatest but the Beatles were the most beautiful. Following pages: Scenes from the Beatles' Florida trip

How did you find America?
We went to Greenland
and made a left turn.

[RINGO]

Ringo: I love him—especially his poems.

What do you do when you're cooped up in a hotel room between shows?
George: Ice skate.

Do you have a message for America?
Paul: Yes, we do actually. Our message is . . . Buy More Beatle Records.

"The Beatles wit," reported *The New York Times*, "was contagious." The reporter, seeking some way to impress his readers with the extraordinary nature of this event, chose an emblem that meant a great deal to any battered veteran of a thousand press conferences: "Photographers," he wrote, "forgot about pictures they wanted to take."

From there it was: on to the Plaza (a staid hotel that had accepted reservations from a group of British businessmen some months before and was not at all happy when they turned out to be John, Paul, George and Ringo); mobs of screaming girls; the broadcast of the Sullivan show; more mobs of screaming girls; a trip to Washington; more screaming; the train back to New York ("Wild-Eyed Mobs Pursue Beatles," headlined the *Times*); the sold-out Carnegie Hall shows, and a flight to Miami.

The Beatles return to Heathrow from America. Prime Minister Sir Alec Douglas-Home called them "our best exports." Mr. Harold Wilson, leader of the Labour Party and a Liverpool MP, accused the Tories of "trying to make the Beatles their secret weapon."

Despite this enthusiasm, the press was not entirely sure just how to cover the Beatles. In most of the early reporting they are described as virtually indistinguishable from each other; even the *Herald Tribune*'s keen-eyed Tom Wolfe described them as "all short slight kids from Liverpool who wear four-button coats, stovepipe pants, ankle-high black boots with Cuban heels. And droll looks on their faces." Perhaps because of this confusion, he also assigned Ringo's remark on Beethoven's poetry to John.

These confusions now seem almost unimaginable—not just because each of the Beatles has so clear an image in our minds, but because the Beatles changed the way popular culture was treated by the American press. Slowly, specialists appeared in the daily papers; "rock critics" began to analyze the music with almost religious seriousness. Finally, and perhaps more important, a new genre of publications appeared as an outlet for these writers. Some of these "underground" journals were short-lived, but all were more than mere "fanzines" on the old, pre-Beatles model. The best of them eventually brought a pop sensibility to the coverage of political events that had once been treated only with the solemnity of the *Times* or the sensationalism of the New York *Daily News*. The loose counterculture network at once created and validated the chain of events

On the set of the Beatles' first film, directed by Richard Lester. The original title, 'Eight Arms to Hold You,' was changed at the end of the shooting, when Ringo said the whole experience had been 'A Hard Day's Night.'

now lumped together as "the Sixties."

But they didn't exist in 1963. And though press coverage of the Beatles was almost universally favorable, it was, as it had been in England, focused on the *event* far more than on the music.

This is not surprising, for the music—as music—was difficult to categorize; when newspapers did attempt to take pop "seriously," the results were often ludicrous. *The New York Times* classics critic Theodore Strongin did observe (in tongue-in-cheek contradistinction to the *London Times* claim) that the Beatles' music was "diatonic," but then dribbled off to note that "three of the four Beatles play different sizes of electron-

The dialogue for the film was written in imitation of the Beatles' Liverpool style. John described it as, "Me, witty. Ringo, dumb and cute." Above and right: Aboard the train hired for the film at Paddington Station. Overleaf: Backstage and off camera, the Beatles in a four-man sweater knit by a fan

ically amplified pluck-string instruments." Jazz critic John S. Wilson, reviewing their Carnegie Hall performances, was even more pusillanimous and contented himself solely with describing the audience. His lengthy story didn't mention any songs by name—presumably, alas, because no critic took pop music seriously enough to learn the titles.

The line was thus drawn not so much between those who thought the Beatles were "cute" and those who thought them "meaningful"—even tin-eared sociologists were willing to grant them importance as a phenomenon—but between two quite different camps: those who listened to the music and those who didn't.

Nowhere was the new line drawn more clearly than among folk music fans. Though centered in New York, the folkies had established outposts (or at least coffee houses) in virtually every college town in America. They were undeniably cultish, finding the popular Kingston Trio *obvious* sell-outs. Still, the folkies' preoccupation with music was a way

'A Hard Day's Night,' a hugely profitable film, was included in a California time capsule to be opened in the year 2960. The film was released and distributed (right) in July 1964. Following pages: Specially designed Beatle dresses worn by the fans (left) for the opening of the film (right)

of extending high school's cultural solidarity and—finally—an anticipation of the rock culture that was about to explode. Yet despite their nostalgia for Woody Guthrie's blue-collar heroes, they scarcely bothered to veil their contempt for contemporary working-class culture. Rock 'n' roll was, as the phrase had it, "pimple music." The more self-righteous among them would never overcome this snobbery, and would certainly never forgive Bob Dylan for failing to be as narrow-minded as they.

Dylan, undoubtedly the central creative force among the Sixties "singer-songwriters," first heard the Beatles over his car radio during a 1964 cross-country drive; he was knocked out: "They were doing things nobody was doing. Their chords were outrageous, just outrageous, and their harmonies made it all valid. . . . Everybody else thought they were for the teenyboppers, that they were gonna pass right away. But it was ob-

We'd all have lovely peaceful lives but for you encouraging them.

[AUNT MIMI TO MRS. HARRISON]

vious to me that they had staying power. I knew they were pointing to the direction where music had to go.'' Not even Brian could have hoped for more.

By the time they returned to England, the Beatles were poised on the cutting edge not merely of a musical moment, but of a generational movement. Clothes, hair, sex, music, drugs, even *The New York Times* . . . nothing

A gala was held after the film's opening. Ringo's Mum (left) said, "It was like a fairy story. It was all lovely." George with Mrs. Harrison (top) and Paul with his family (above)

121

after the Beatles would ever be quite the same as it had been before.

The Beatles returned to England as conquering heroes; Epstein's monumental gamble had paid off in his home country as well, and the prime minister praised their "useful contribution to the country's balance of payments." They did not, however, rest on their laurels.

In March, two weeks after their return, John published his first book, *In His Own Write*. Though readers of the *Mersey Beat* had long been aware that his skill with words extended well beyond the odd "yeah, yeah, yeah" (his pseudonymous "Beatcomber" column was the only part of the paper that can fairly be described as having a style), the

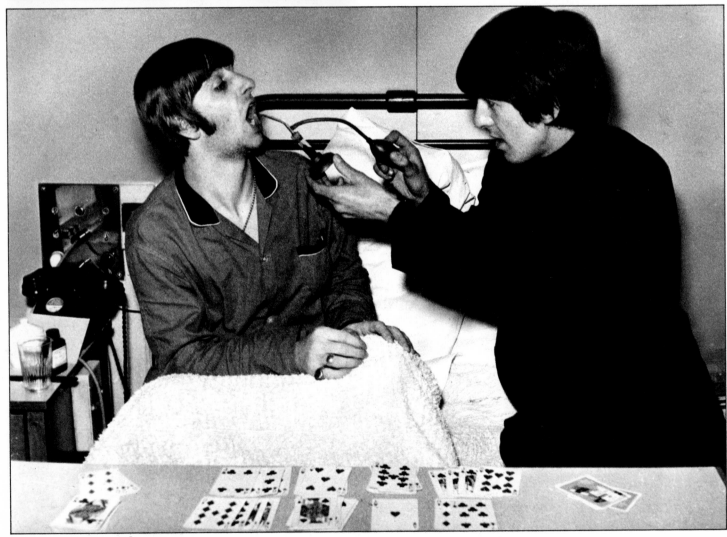

When Ringo came down with tonsillitis (above), Jimmy Nicol (top) subbed as drummer on the Beatles' 1964 European tour.

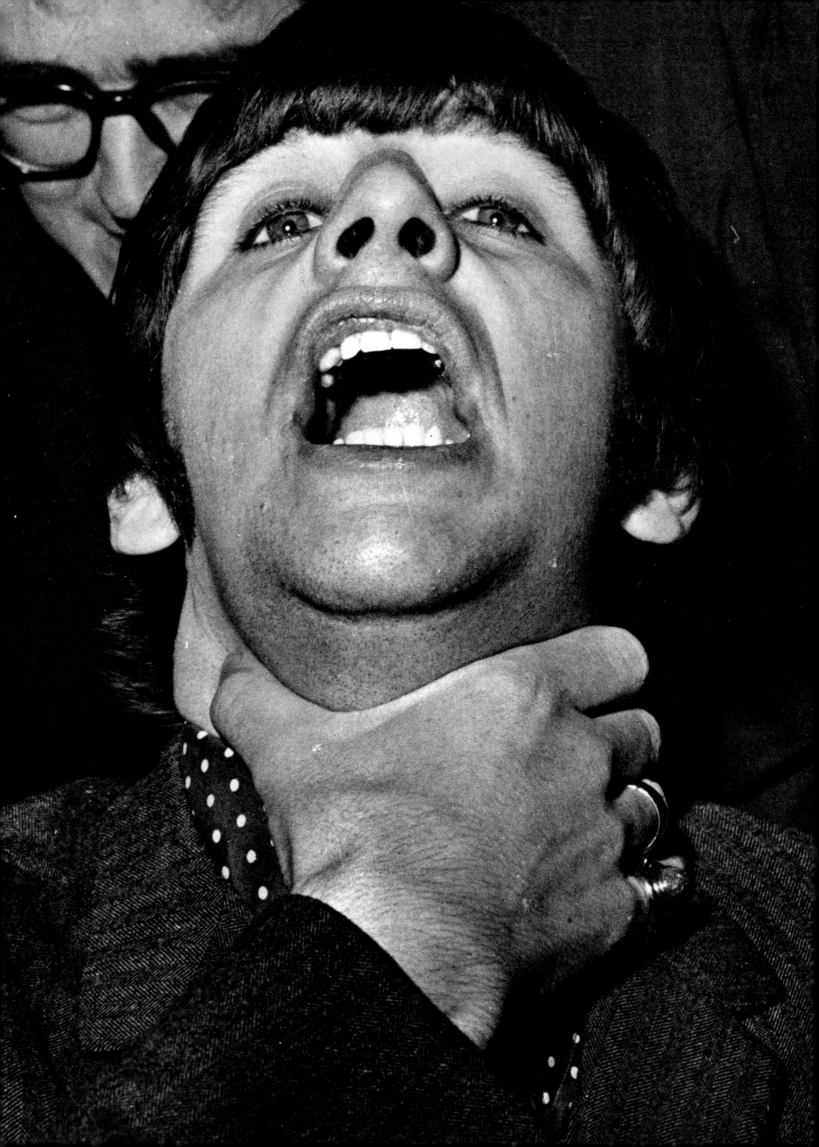

rest of England was unprepared for him. The collection of playful stories and slight sketches embracing such cheery themes as domestic murder, cannibalism and race hatred came as both surprise and delight. The *Times Literary Supplement* observed that the book was "worth the attention of anyone who fears for the impoverishment of the English language and the British imagination." It sold more than 300,000 copies in England and was also a best seller in America, where a *Newsweek* reviewer—less concerned than the *TLS* about the future of the British imagination—correctly noted that the book "suggests that when John Lennon sings 'I Want to Hold Your Hand,' he is wishing he could bite it."

Oh yes, they also had another number-one record in March—"Can't Buy Me Love," which Paul and John had written on their way to tape an Ed Sullivan show in Miami. And then they went into the film studio.

Nothing in their early career so firmly

Maureen Cox was 17 when she went on a holiday with Ringo, Paul, and Jane Asher. Shockwaves of moral indignation rocked England, although her father said, "I have every confidence in her good judgment." Overleaf: The Beatles' triumphant return to Liverpool in July 1964

fixed their images or broadened their audiences as *A Hard Day's Night*. The film, whose low ($600,000) budget had been fixed before the Beatles hit superstardom, was anything but sumptuous. Shot in black and white rather than color, and filled with all the camera-spinning tricks of *nouvelle vague*, it was a manic pseudodocumentary of a "typical" Beatles day. Mostly, they flee from their fans and are cheeky to their elders (who always deserve it). At its best, the film perfectly conveys the message the Beatles were sending in their songs—they were a little out of place in this world, but that just might be the world's fault rather than theirs.

Following its glittering Royal premiere in London that July, *A Hard Day's Night* went on to become a huge financial success—and still stands as one of the largest grossing films, relative to investment, in history. If anything, its critical success was even more striking, for it forced a generation that had automatically disdained the Beatles to take them seriously as artists. Consider the vaguely dis-

The Beatles and the Lord Mayor wave to the crowd of 100,000 from the balcony of the Liverpool Town Hall. On George's 21st birthday, Mrs. Harrison had to call special postal vans to take away the overflow of fan letters being delivered above.

Touring was murder. We hardly saw anything because we had to stay inside hotel rooms all the time. And we were always dead beat.

[RINGO]

believing tone of these rapturous American reviews:

"With all the ill will in the world, one sits there, watching and listening—and feels one's intelligence dissolving in a pool of approbation."—*Newsweek*

"This is going to surprise you—it may knock you right out of your chair—but the new film with those incredible chaps, the Beatles, is a whale of a comedy. . . . I wouldn't believe it either if I hadn't seen it with my own astonished eyes . . ."—Bosley Crowther, *The New York Times*

"One approached the Beatles with apprehension, knowing only the idiotic hairdo and the melancholy wail. [But] . . . *A Hard Day's Night* is a smart and stylish film, exhilarating in its audacity and modernity."—Arthur Schlesinger Jr., *Show Magazine*

As *A Hard Day's Night* was still packing them into first-run theaters across the country, the Beatles began their "real" American tour (the first whirlwind visit had been essentially a publicity stunt). This time, the month-long extravaganza included stops in twenty-four cities. It was originally supposed to be only twenty-three, opening in San Francisco and working east, but Kansas City was added to the tour when Charles O Finley —more generous with the Beatles than with his baseball players—offered them an astonishing $150,000 for a single show. They could have done without it, thank you, but Epstein recognized the publicity value of the offer and persuaded them to accept. Other promoters didn't relish the news, however, and *Variety* noted that "another factor causing unhappiness at the Beatles is the fact that many native headliners have started demanding the same kind of coin. It is an open secret that shortly after the Beatles inked their first deal calling for $25,000 guaranteed against sixty percent of the gross, Bob Hope demanded the same kind of deal. Previously his dates were predicated on a guarantee of around $15,000."

After a while, no money would seem enough, for the touring made them prisoners. Ostensibly available to their fans, they were in fact sealed off from the world. Their hotels were besieged, their getaway cars mobbed. Despite—or perhaps because of—the interchangeable parade of groupies, their lives became one indistinguishable hotel room, with cabin fever its invariable accompaniment.

But they were trapped by more than circumstances, for the times themselves made them hypocrites. Thinking back on the lovable lads of *A Hard Day's Night*, one has to struggle to remember just who their real-life counterparts were. As John remembers, "I mean, we had this one image, but man, our tours were like something else . . . the Beatles tours were like Fellini's *Satyricon*." These were four increasingly mean, amphetamine-gobbling, gonzo drunks. Who had to make nice to everyone.

The Mayor of Whozis wanted his picture taken with Ringo? Swell. Nothing the boys would like better. Radio WWWW wanted a quick interview with John? Of course. No trouble at all. Just wait till we extract the Mayor of Whozis' teenage daughter from his shower, okay? Whozis' polyester DJ version of the Fifth Beatle wanted an exclusive with Paul? Absolutely. Tell him to bring the pills to Room 1633—and this time he should bring a couple of extra girls for the roadies, too. Sorry, no interviews with George. He's too busy throwing up right now.

They had, at once, no private lives at all and lives their excesses made so private that no unapproved human contact was ever al-

On their American tour (left), the Beatles travelled 22,441 miles, flew 60 hours, visited 24 cities and gave 31 performances in 32 days. Above: Brian with the boys. Following pages: Las Vegas; Los Angeles, where Jayne Mansfield (page 136) joins them at the Whiskey à Go Go.

The following eight pages contain pictures of the memorabilia lovingly collected over the past twenty years by Beatles fans. (1) 'A Hard Day's Night,' released June 1964, (2) suitcase-hat box, (3) 'The Early Beatles,' released March 1965, (4) penny banks, (5) sneakers, (6) ticket to the last live concert in Candlestick Park, San Francisco, August 9th, 1966, and tags promoting Beatles movies, (7) necklace with Beatles medallion, (8) 'Sgt. Pepper's Lonely Hearts Club Band,' June 1967, (9), (10), (11) buttons, (12) 'The Beatles vs. the Four Seasons,' released on Vee Jay, October 1964, (13) Yellow Submarine lunchbox, (14) the German release of 'Please Please Me,' (15) 'The Beatles' Story,' released November 1964, (16) serving tray, (17) Yellow Submarine water-color set and Beatles pin-ups, (18) 'Yellow Submarine,' released January 1969, (19) rings, (20) harmonica, (21) bubblegum cards, (22) 'The Amazing Beatles,' (23) original album cover for ' "Yesterday" . . . and Today' (reacting to the dismembering of their British albums by Capitol in the U.S., the Beatles posed as butchers for this picture. Capitol replaced the cover at their own expense. It cost $200,000), (24) the final cover to ' "Yesterday" . . . and Today,' released June 1966, (25) patch, (26) 'Magical Mystery Tour,' released November 1967, (27) wallpaper, (28) painted water glass, (29) button, (30) tie-tac pinned to Beatle cardboard backing, (31) carrying case for 45-rpm records, (32) John stamps, (33) Yellow Submarine jigsaw puzzle, (34) Christmas calendar from Japan, (35) early poster pullout from English fan magazine, (36) promotional Band-Aid from 'Help!', (37) belt, (38) figurines with bobbing heads, (39) key rings, (40) lunchbox, (41) 'Beatles '65,' released December 1964, (42) 'I Want to Hold Your Hand,' released as a single January 1964, (43) wristwatch, (44) 'Rubber Soul,' released December 1965, (Continued on page 135)

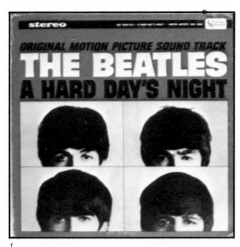

1

2

3

4

5

6

7

8

9

10

11

12

13

14

15

16

17

18

19

20

21

22

23

24

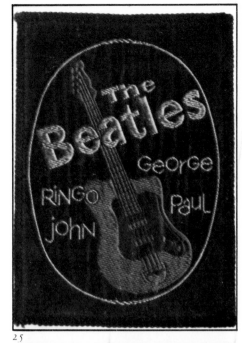

25

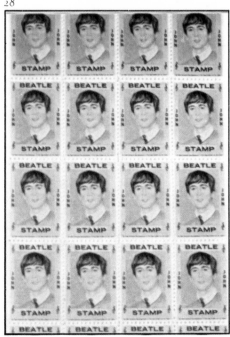

28

26

29

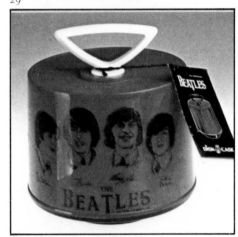

31

33

27

30

32

34

35

36

37

38

39

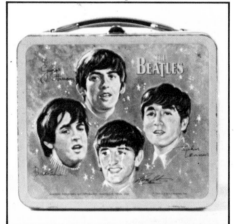

40

41

42

43

44

45

46

47

48

49

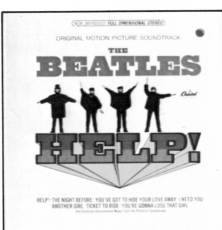

50

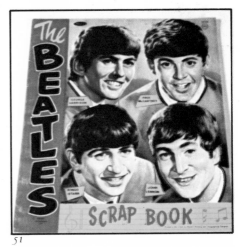

51

52

53

54

57

55

PERSONALITY BATH

60

56

I'M A BEATLE FAN In Case of EMERGENCY CALL PAUL OR RINGO

58

61

59

62

63

64

65

66

67

68

69

70

71

72

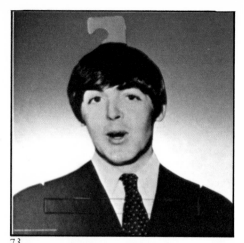

73

74

75

76

77

78

79

80

81

82

83

(45) poster announcing producer Sid Bernstein's summer concerts for 1965, including the Beatles at Shea Stadium on August 15th, (46) promotional postcard from 'Help!', (47) Shea Stadium poster, Tuesday, August 23rd, 1966, (48) buttons and guitar pins, (49) wallet, (50) 'Help!', released August 1965, (51) scrapbook, (52) patch, (53) pillows, (54) pencil case with zipper, (55) Japanese calendar featuring a photo from 'Help!' with an Austrian stand-in for Ringo, (56) two books by John: 'In His Own Write,' 1964, and 'A Spaniard in the Works,' 1965, (57) 'The Beatles Book,' a British monthly fan magazine published while the Beatles were together, (58) button, (59) movie tickets, (60) bubble bath, (61) 'At the Hollywood Bowl' record, (62) 'Something New,' released June 1964, (63) gold medal commemorating 1964 tour to the U.S., (64) loose-leaf notebook, (65) promotional stand for record stores, with electrical bobbing heads, (66) plastic dolls, (67) 'The Beatles' Second Album,' released April 1964, (68) Beatle patches, (69) 'Beatles VI,' released June 1965, (70) concert tickets, (71) buttons for Britain's first Beatle convention, (72) bubblegum cards and postcards, (73) Paul coat hanger, (74) button, (75) 'Abbey Road,' released October 1969, (76) 'Hey Jude,' released February 1970, (77) apple crate for Apple records, (78) and (79) buttons urging the Beatles back, which began to appear in the early 1970s, (80) 'Revolver,' released August 1966, (81) 'Let It Be,' released May 1970, (82) poster for Rock 'n' Roll Music, released June 1976, (83) buttons.

The commotion doesn't bother us anymore. It's like working in a bell factory. You don't hear the bells anymore.
[PAUL]

lowed to reach them. The approved ones—journalists—all asked the same questions anyway, and the answers began to emerge as sincerely as a candidate's smile. Long before their weepy successors would compose mournful and profitable laments about the travails of touring, the Beatles were sick of it.

Most seriously, they were worried about their music. They felt themselves to be at their most fertile, but the music wasn't developing. Indeed, it often seemed to be decaying. In Hamburg, their eight-hour nights had forced them to change and grow; even their first theater tour of England gave them hour-long sets to play with. But the world

"It was wrecking our playing. The noise of the people just drowned everything," said Ringo. "Eventually I just played off the beat. I couldn't hear myself half the time." Atlantic City (above), and Dallas (right)

tours were different. Shows were kept strictly in the half-hour range, and the song sequence was identical night after night. Under the best of circumstances they would have grown stale, but these tours didn't even offer decent working conditions. The hotels and the air travel were first class, but the audio equipment was primitive in the extreme. The Beatles regularly played giant stadiums using equipment that a self-respecting bar band would reject today.

They had no choice. Because the Beatles invented the rock 'n' roll tour on this scale, the technology to support it simply didn't exist. They worked, for instance, without monitors, and between the screaming crowds and their heavily boosted amplifiers, they were often completely unable to hear each other. They lost the beat, they sang off key, they said the hell with it and just mimed the words. But nobody cared; they were the Beatles.

Ringo (left): "I'm not very good at singing, so they write songs for me that are pretty low and not too hard." Paul and John (above): "Neither of us can read or write music. John will whistle at me," Paul said, "and I'll whistle back at him."

Thus, though the constant whirr and click of cameras accompanied the public Beatles, the important musical developments of their touring years took place offstage. During those early tours, the Beatles were a rock 'n' roll band: The beat was everything. George's lead guitar was buried deep in the mix, often limited to fills, and the dominant sound featured John's driving riffs and Ringo's cymbals. The vocal harmonies were more unusual (the Everly Brothers meet Little Richard meet the Dell-Vikings and gobble down speed together), but the lead track was often recorded by two or three voices singing in unison; the result was so dense that it became a fans' party game to guess who sang what. Finally, though the early albums are remarkable for their relatively small percentage of

filler, producer George Martin was forced to record them in what now seems an unconscionable hurry; listen, for instance, to the voices going flat in "Hold Me Tight," on their second album.

But they were recorded—and even more remarkably, bought—as *albums*, not as one or two hit singles padded out with B-sides and covers of other singers' work. Though these early albums seem almost perversely simple in the light of *Sgt. Pepper* or *Revolver*, they nonetheless redefined the music market. Before the Beatles, the conventional wisdom had argued that kids bought singles and adults bought albums. The big money—for lush productions with Percy Faith's strings and the Ray Charles Singers oohing in the background—thus went to "adult" artists like Perry Como and Patti Page.

The Beatles, recording their own songs and the classics of an earlier generation, had begun to change these marketing assumptions even before *A Hard Day's Night*; from then on, however, they began spending more time in the studio, and their work gradually changed as their range expanded to the limits of recording technology. Their last 1964 single, "I Feel Fine," opened with the insistent buzz of guitar feedback and faded to the accompaniment of barking dogs. But the song went number one in both England and America, giving them the confidence to continue their experiments. Before they could get back to the studios, however, they spent four months filming their next picture, *Help!*, which would be released in July 1965. But they returned to England in June, in time for the announcement that the Queen would award them the MBE (Member of the Order of the British Empire) for their services to

When I first went out with Ritchie (Ringo) I had to be careful because of the fans. I might easily have been killed otherwise.

[MAUREEN COX STARKEY]

British commerce.

This touched off a splendid row of the sort that one thought existed only in *Punch* cartoons of stuffy old clubmen. Not so. (Or, in any case, a clear instance of life imitating art.) Many former MBEs were moved to return their medals in a huff, and one, a retired lieutenant colonel, even wrote the Labour Party out of his will. Canadian MP Hector Dupuis spoke for this group when he wrote that he thought war heroes shouldn't be put "on the same level as vulgar nincompoops."

At the height of Beatlemania (left), Ringo married Maureen. Above: Brian embraces them both. Following pages: Mr. and Mrs. Richard Starkey on the day after their wedding, and with John and Cynthia in Tobago. "I don't think women like to be equal," said Ringo. "They like to be protected and in turn they like looking after men. That's how it is."

George suggested that if Dupuis didn't want his medal, "he had better give it back to us. Then we can give it to our manager, Brian Epstein. MBE really stands for 'Mr. Brian Epstein.'"

Epstein seemed more thrilled by the award than the Beatles were; John, at least, had to be persuaded that accepting the award didn't violate some principle or other. But after the October ceremony, which gave him his second chance to observe royalty close up, even he couldn't help sounding slightly impressed: "I really think," he said, "the Queen believes it all. She must. I don't believe in John Lennon, Beatle, being any different from anybody else, because I know he's not. I'm just a feller. But I'm sure the Queen must think she's different." He also, alert readers will have noticed, sounded slightly stoned. This is because the Fab Four's bravado had temporarily deserted them before their meeting with the Queen, and they'd retired to a Buckingham Palace bathroom for a hasty joint.

But they managed, despite a few misplaced giggles, to get through the ceremony with the dignity of the Crown and Liverpool mu-

Above, right and following pages: Scenes from 'Help!' shot in England, Austria and the Bahamas. Paul admitted 'Help!' "wasn't our film. We were sort of guest stars. It was fun, but basically as an idea for a film it was a bit wrong for us."

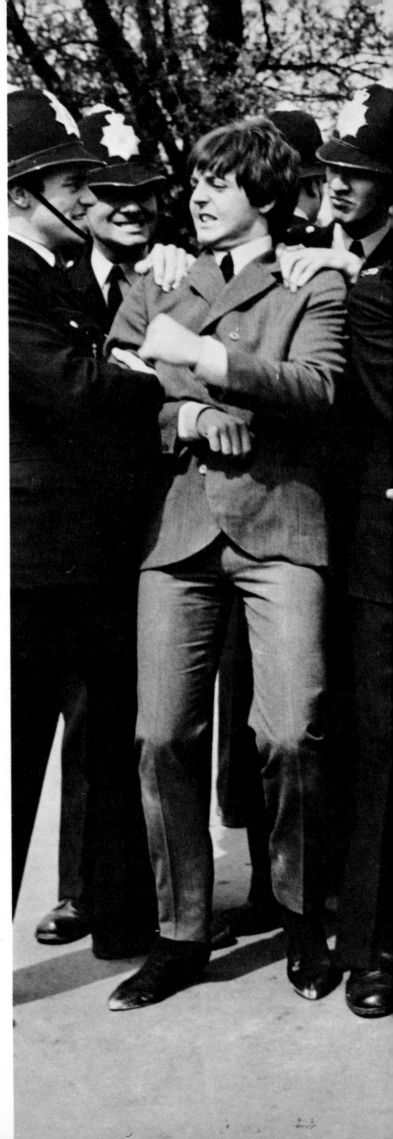

tually unimpaired.

The fuss over the MBE announcement was temporarily eclipsed when they left for a summer tour of France, Italy and Spain, where they received the by-now-usual adulation. While they were out of the country, John's second book, *A Spaniard in the Works*, made its appearance. Like his first, it became an almost instant best seller, but despite some wonderful creations—especially Jesus El Pifco, a "garlic-eating, little yellow greasy fascist"—the book seemed a little flat, lacking the element of surprise that had made *In His Own Write* seem so special.

Much the same fate befell *Help!* when it was released—with the important difference that it really wasn't up to its predecessor's standard. It was fun—the send-up of James Bond allowed for some lovely chase scenes, and Leo McKern was a spectacularly despicable villain—but that's all.

It wasn't enough, for away from the rarified atmosphere of Beatlemania, pop music was in the process of becoming a little more than fun. The transition was best signalled by the Byrds, a West Coast group of folkies manqués, whom *Newsweek* described as "Dylanized Beatles"; critic Lillian Roxon rightly corrected the direction of the flow when she observed that, "the whole point is that they're Beatlized Dylans." If the Beatles had legitimized rock 'n' roll's form, the Byrds legitimized its content, and in their wake, a whole series of American rivals to the Beatles' throne emerged.

Some of these new figures were veterans of the New York City folk scene, but on the West Coast, the Doors uttered their muscular, mysterious threats, and even the Beach Boys threatened to abandon their little deuce

coupe for the sublime confusions of *Smile*. The seal was stamped on the change when Bob Dylan outraged his fans and "went electric."

The summer of 1965 was an extraordinary musical season, surely the best since the heyday of Elvis and Buddy Holly. Among its hit singles were the Byrds' "Mr. Tambourine Man," the Rolling Stones' "Satisfaction," the Beatles' "Ticket to Ride," and Dylan's "Like a Rolling Stone." Rock 'n' roll became rock that year; suddenly the Beatles— still churning out "Dizzy Miss Lizzie" and "Can't Buy Me Love" to screaming girls at Shea Stadium—seemed to be singing silly love songs. Nevertheless, they were the new music's seminal force; critic Robert Christgau, writing in 1973, gave them their due when he defined "rock" as "all music deriving primarily from the energy and influence of the Beatles—and maybe Bob Dylan, and maybe you should stick pretensions in there someplace."

Toward the end of 1965, the Beatles once again entered the studio, emerging from it

Above: Paul and George before the Shea Stadium concert, 1965. Left and following pages: Shea Stadium broke all attendance records. Tickets sold out immediately. "The greatest gross ever in the history of show business," said Sid Bernstein, the promoter. The performers arrived by helicopter and armored car. The fans' screams cancelled out the music. Not only were the Beatles inaudible, they were almost invisible, as the stage was set way out at second base.

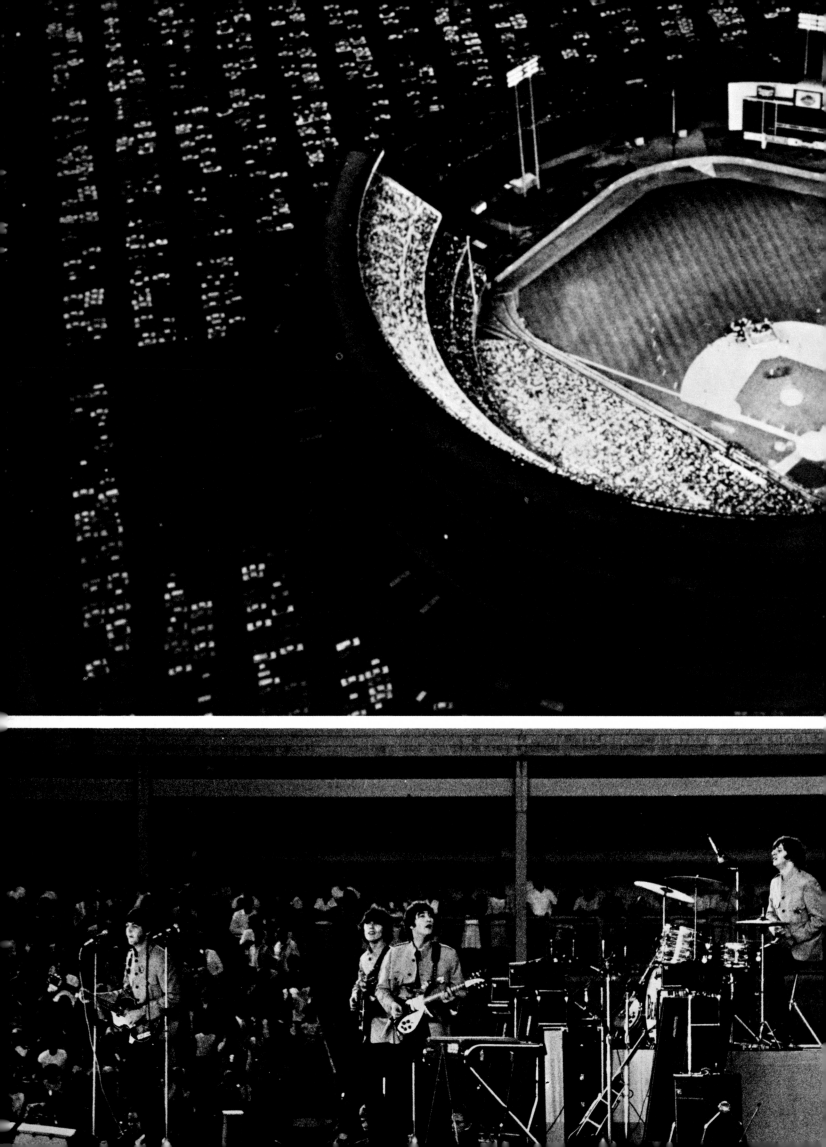

far ahead of their rivals. That year's Christmas release, *Rubber Soul*, is arguably their finest album. Though they would continue touring through the next summer, *Rubber Soul* was a watershed. It was more than just an affirmation that they weren't through—though it was certainly that—it was also the new standard against which subsequent albums by pretenders to the throne would be measured. The pumping acoustic drive of "I've Just Seen a Face," the eerie allusiveness of "Norwegian Wood," the simple warmth of "In My Life," the stunning modulations of "You Won't See Me" . . . all delivered with an instrumental virtuosity and richness that had only been hinted at in the earlier albums.

Fifteen years after the fact, only Paul's "Michelle" seems a mistake (and what the hell, even John sang "I need money"). Without losing their enthusiasm, the Beatles had given *Rubber Soul* a depth and texture that had long been missing from pop sensibility.

This album was the most persuasive argument that their future lay in the studio rather than on tour, but they had miles to go before they slept. In the summer of 1966, following the release of "*Yesterday*" . . . *and Today*—an album closer in spirit to *Help!* and *Beatles VI* than to *Rubber Soul*—they toured Germany, Japan, Manila and the United States.

They were, by this time, musical schizophrenics. Their imaginations were stretching

Above: Maureen Cox Starkey, Cynthia Powell Lennon, Patti Boyd (soon to be Mrs. George Harrison). Cynthia wrote, "We always knew the Beatles came first and the wives second. Theirs was a marriage of three guitars and a drum. We were the little women trying to cope." Right: John done up as Elvis for a party. Following pages: Paul in the makeup room and the Beatles rehearsing for a British TV show.

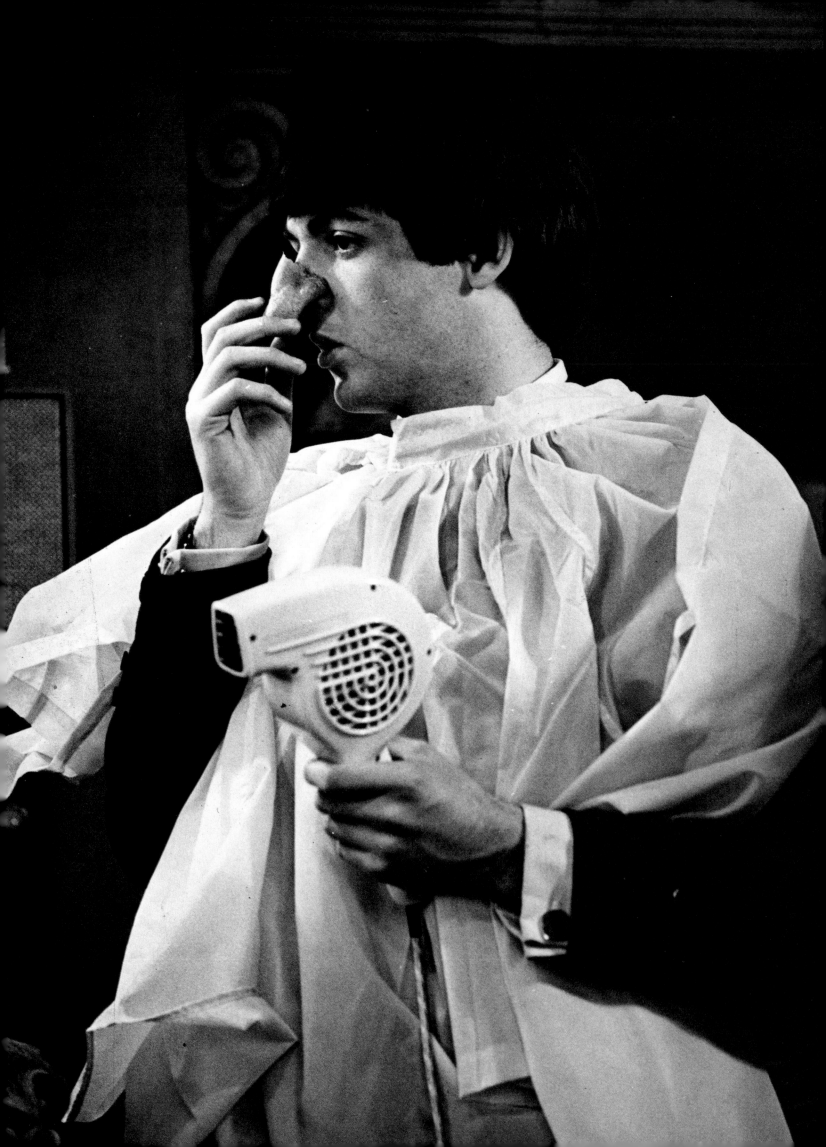

It's a keen pad. The Queen? She was just like a mum to us.

[PAUL]

forward to *Revolver* and *Sgt. Pepper*, yet they still had fans who longed to shriek and throw jellybeans. In this, the band paid the penalty for being pioneers.

Because the Beatles had gone first—had *created* a rock audience—succeeding groups were no longer expected to please the teenyboppers and the intellectuals simultaneously. Most of them had the luxury of specializing, and virtually all took advantage of it. Thus if the Monkees zeroed in on teenage America (and got sneered at for their trouble), groups like the Jefferson Airplane, the Rolling Stones and the Who were definitely not expected to be all cute and cuddly. The Beatles, still struggling to do everything at once, had to weather comments like Hunter Thompson's gratuitous observation that "The Rolling Stones want to pillage your town, but the Beatles just want to hold your hand."

Perhaps even more annoying, their role as models for the world's youth—something not even the most crazed publicist would ever attempt to assign to the Rolling Stones —left them open for attacks from the non-musical world as well. This, at the same time American critics were complaining that "*Yesterday*" . . . *and Today* was a step backward (it

The Beatles were made Members of the British Empire in 1965. Throngs of heaving, shoving fans brought traffic to a halt as the boys arrived at Buckingham Palace. "We had to curtsy when we met the Queen," said John. "We just had a giggle."

Four Young Singers Pay a Call on the Queen and Look What Happens

London policemen struggling to control Beatle fans outside Buckingham Palace yesterday while, inside, the cause of all this, the Beatles, were being made Members of the Order of the British Empire for services to their country.

United Press International Cablephotos

And here they are, M.B.E.'s and all, from left: Paul McCartney, George Harrison, John Lennon and Ringo Starr. Beatles were among 180 persons who were awarded by Queen.

JOHN, PAUL, RINGO AND GEORGE, M.B.E.

Beatles Honored by Queen at Her 'Keen Pad' as Band Plays 'Humoresque'

By DANA ADAMS SCHMIDT

Special to The New York Times

LONDON, Oct. 26 — The Beatles, in dark suits and ties, stood still long enough today for Queen Elizabeth II to make them Members of the Order of the British Empire. There were reports that Ringo had had a haircut for the occasion.

George Harrison, John Lennon, Paul McCartney and Ringo Starr, standing solemnly in a row, received the award, the lowest of five divisions of the order, for service to their country.

As the Queen pinned the medals on their narrow lapels, she asked, "How long have you been together now?"

"Oh, for many years," said Paul.

"Forty years," said Ringo, and everybody laughed. The group started in the fifties.

"Are you the one that started it all?" the Queen asked Ringo.

Ringo said the others had started it.

"I'm the little one," he said.

Queen in Gold Gown

The Queen, in a pale gold gown, presented the medals in Buckingham Palace in a cream-and-gold room with an organ at one end and six chandeliers overhead.

"A keen pad," Paul said later.

The band of the Coldstream Guards daintily played tunes from "Bitter Sweet" and "Humoresque."

The Lord Chamberlain, Lord Cobbold, first read out the Beatles' names. The four stepped forward four paces and bowed. The Queen shook hands, spoke to each and pinned on the medals. Then the four took four steps back, and bowed again.

Speaking of the Queen later, Paul said:

"She's lovely, great. She was very friendly. She was just like a mum to us."

George related that the Queen was "sort of motherly and smiling to put us at our ease."

180 Get Awards

The Beatles were among 180 persons who received awards at today's investiture, including six who were knighted. The awards were announced in Queen Elizabeth's Birthday Honors list last June.

Apart from having become probably the most popular British singers ever, the Beatles have brought many millions of pounds into the British Treasury from their recordings and movies.

Although other entertainers have often been honored, the awards to these pop singers, two of whom are 22 years old and two 24, brought numerous letters of protest. Two holders of the M.B.E., a former member of Parliament and a former Royal Air Force squadron leader, returned their medals to the Queen.

The award entitles the Beatles to put the letters M.B.E. after their names. According to Debrett's, the standard reference on such matters, the M.B.E. ranks 120th in the 126 titles of precedence. It is the most widely given honor.

Four thousand Beatle fans outside Buckingham Palace were not overawed. Their squeals and chants of "Yeah, Yeah, Yeah" downed out the pipes of the Scots Guards and the band of the Grenadier Guards. Policemen linked arms to hold them back, but could not prevent them from climbing the gates and lampposts.

Quotation of the Day

"She was just like a mum to us."—Paul McCartney, after Queen Elizabeth II had pinned the Most Excellent Order of the British Empire on the Beatles at Buckingham Palace. [This Page, Column 8.]

RED IVE

lead
ive
d

, N. Y.,
ssioner
is city
t more
in the
ert Fay
rth Ave-
rch, that
is flour-

st a few
d Hill is
t for glar-
efore the
the com-

sed the
t of the
e in ar-
okmak-
ick re-

com-
r-old
nter-
est-
a
le
y

of
other
ed to
ses to
Carey,
e gam-
ct, and
an West-
ials. Con-
any impor-
he obtains
r to United
bert M. Mor-
ral agents.
ted that every
r reported by
arrested by
the last year
d the evidence
Federal files.
t gambling
Rochelle.
e in-
came
150
of
all

---

yer, 35, Gets Key Post | Army for International Affairs, replaces Joseph A. Califano Jr., now a special assistant to President Johnson. | **U.S. Takes Over Memorial** WASHINGTON, Oct. 26 — ustus Saint- n Cornish.

Namara's Assistant

Oct. 26 (AP)

U.S. aides decry emphasis 'v retirement

Big Board's public disclosu examined

wasn't really a step at all, just a hasty American repackaging of British singles and album outtakes), the right wing was recognizing their importance. As the emotional force of rock 'n' roll blended with the emerging political force that would come to be described as the Movement, the right wing found communists lurking beneath the Fab Four's amplifiers. Those cheerful chipmunks from Let Freedom Ring (an Indiana offshoot of the John Birch Society) denounced the Beatles' "destructive process," claiming that, "Communist scientists have discovered that music with a broken meter in the treble, played over an insistently regular beat which increases to the point of frenzy, can produce hysterical effects in young people, as if they were trying to rush madly in two directions at once." This trenchant analysis was, er, amplified by a touring minister from Billy Hargis' Christian Crusade. Warning that "the drum is the key—little Ringo," the Reverend David Noebel galvanized congregations with the threat that "in the excitatory state that the Beatles place these youngsters into, these young people will do anything they are told to do. . . . One day when the revolution is ripe, the communists could put the Beatles on TV and could mass hypnotize American youth. This," he concluded in a statement that was all too obviously true, "scares the wits out of me."

These slings and arrows were more amusing than painful; they certainly didn't seem to have any effects on the ever-growing crowds who turned out to see the Beatles dur-

The Beatles display the MBEs (left) that caused an uproar among British war heroes. Medals were returned to Buckingham Palace. John said, "I thought the MBE was for killing people. Ours is for entertaining them. I'd say we deserved it more, wouldn't you?" Following pages: Crowds of fainting teenage girls were laid out shoulder to shoulder on the pavement. A shuttle service of ambulances took the injured to the hospital.

The friendship of Paul and Jane lasted five years. She, unlike the Beatle wives, kept her independence as an actress. Top: George and Patti on their wedding day. "George is my husband," she said, "but he's got to be free to go with the others if he wants." Above: John with Cynthia in Paris.

ing their tours. But during the Manila stop on their summer 1966 tour of the Far East, they faced a riot of a considerably less friendly variety than those they'd experienced before.

Their screaming American fans might have wanted to tear the buttons from their clothes, but the Filipinos wanted to dismember them. They had, it seems, slighted President Marcos' wife by failing to attend a luncheon at the Presidential Palace. They claimed they'd never gotten the invitation, but Mrs. Marcos certainly treated their no-show as a wanton attack on Philippine honor. With the government-controlled police curiously inactive, throngs of students kicked and punched at the Beatles as they ran to their airplane. Later

Above and right: During the 1966 summer tour, the Beatles performed for an audience of 9000 at the Budokan, Tokyo's judo arena.

I don't intend to be a
performing flea anymore.

[JOHN]

on, President Marcos apologized for the "breach of hospitality"; John, ever the diplomat, responded, "I didn't even know they had a president."

It was another Lennonism that provided the more bizarre running story that dogged the Beatles through America during the summer of 1966. Back in February, in an interview with Maureen Cleave of the *London Evening Standard*, John had said, "Christianity will go. It will vanish and shrink. I needn't argue about that, I'm right and will be proved right. We're more popular than Jesus Christ right now." While these comments went

down smoothly enough in the middle of a serious newspaper piece, they jumped right off the page when they were reprinted shortly before the U.S. tour by a pulpy teenage magazine called *Datebook*. Hot diggity! The sort of folks who had always known the Beatles were Commies were delighted to be appalled by this confirmation that they were godless atheists as well.

In the face of radio stations banning Beatle records (mostly in the South, though Boston's WEEI also jumped on the bandwagon) and the promise of giant "Beatle bonfires," Brian Epstein scurried across the ocean to speak soothing words. His first words, however, were more confusing than helpful; as he explained the matter to the *New York Post*, John's remark was "serious to the extent that he'd been misinterpreted." The tempest eventually died down when John made a press conference apology that was accepted in absentia by the Vatican's official newspaper, *L'Osservatore Romano*. (A more impressive celestial editorial, however, was the lightning bolt that knocked Texas station KLUE off the air after it had organized a bonfire of Beatle records.) In retrospect, the comments made against the Vietnam War by all four Beatles during that same press conference seem far more important. Regardless of the cause—and John's remark certainly can't be discounted—attendance on the 1966 tour dipped slightly from the previous year. Even in New York City, hardly a hotbed of fundamentalist Christianity, there were empty

---

Above left: 3000 police kept order at the Tokyo concert, while rightists demonstrated in the street outside (right). Though Beatlemania was still strong (top and overleaf), the Beatles were getting tired. "There were good nights and bad nights on the tours," said Ringo. "But they were really all the same. The only fun part was the hotels in the evening, smoking pot and all that."

Francisco and gave, on August 29th, 1966, their last stage performance ever.

The KYA-Radio DJs who emceed the concert didn't realize they were in on the last show; Brian, who had hoped to reverse the band's decision, insisted that it not be revealed until he'd had the chance to notify their long-time British promoter. By all accounts, however, the last Beatles concert was as musically lackluster as those that had preceded it. They were tired—they'd fought and fucked their way across a continent, using their getaway cars to escape all but a select few of their female fans—and they were bored. Even Ringo, who has called those years "the best time of my life," admitted the frustrations, describing it as "twenty-four hours a day, without a break. Press, people fighting to get into your hotel room, climbing twenty-five stories up drainpipes . . . if it had carried on, I would have gone insane."

Finally, they had outgrown the music their live fans demanded. A rundown of the songs they played during that summer's tour is instructive, for it is full of the "I" "Love" "You" "Want" "Need" "Miss" "Lips" themes they'd been playing with when Paul and John were high school boys. Even if they'd been able to hear themselves on stage —and even if they hadn't begun to suffer a fatal contempt for their too-easily pleased audiences—it was time for them to stop. They could never again be the band they had once been and, in this case at least, they got out gracefully. □

seats at Shea Stadium. And though two teenage girls from Staten Island threatened to jump from the twenty-second floor of a midtown hotel unless they were allowed to see the Beatles (after a half-hour of coaxing, police grabbed them and sent them to a nearby hospital for treatment), there were only nine teenage girls making up the crowd that had waited for the band at the airport.

But they slogged on across the country, answering questions about Christianity at every turn, until they finally reached San

Upper left: Ringo and Maureen with their son Jason, born August 19th, 1967. Lower left: Paul and Jane Asher at Paul's farm in Northern Scotland. Right: In the summer of 1966, when John was quoted as saying, "The Beatles are more popular than Jesus Christ," there were public burnings of Beatle records all through the American Bible Belt. Here, the radio station in Waycross, Georgia, is broadcasting the ceremony. Following pages: 1967

These musical reasons why touring had grown increasingly meaningless to the Beatles became obvious with *Revolver*. The album, released immediately after their tour had ended, raised *Rubber Soul*'s ante considerably: It was virtually unreproducible on stage. The contextual gap between their old music and their new continued to widen—as Paul said, "You don't write fifteen-year-old songs when you're twenty, because you don't think fifteen-year-old thoughts." But it was the technological changes that made *Revolver* a shock —Paul again: "These are sounds that nobody else has done yet...I mean nobody...ever."

Well, maybe. Certainly they were sounds the Beatles hadn't produced before; indeed, "Yellow Submarine," the single that had been pulled from the album to coincide with their final tour, is almost without Beatles music. There is an exceedingly simple bass-and-drum line augmented with acoustic chords, but the "music" is really provided by a weird assortment of sound effects—brass bands, ocean waves and glassware. Its flip side, "Eleanor Rigby," doesn't use the band at all, but a string octet orchestrated by George Martin.

After touring, the Beatles settled down to enjoy their money. "We'd rather be rich than famous," John said. "That is, more rich and slightly less famous." This stage in their careers coincided with the psychedelic era marked by exotic drugs and flamboyant styles. Above: The medicine cabinet in John's study reads SAFE AS MILK, and his conservative old Rolls-Royce (right) got a new coat of paint while the Beatles were recording 'Sgt. Pepper.' Following pages: Long gone are Brian's suits and ties. One commentator described the look of the times as, "Art Nouveau and psychedelic, Op and Pop, Dada and Surrealist, Hieronymus Bosch and just plain bosh."

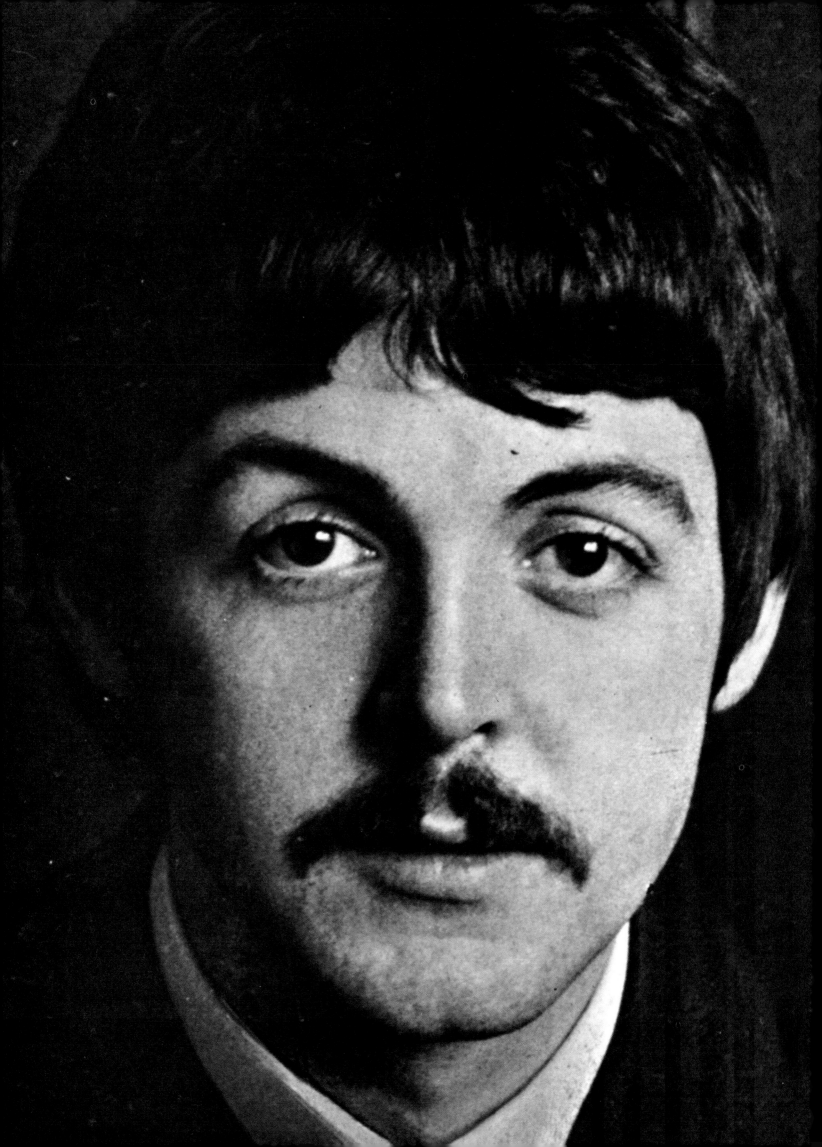

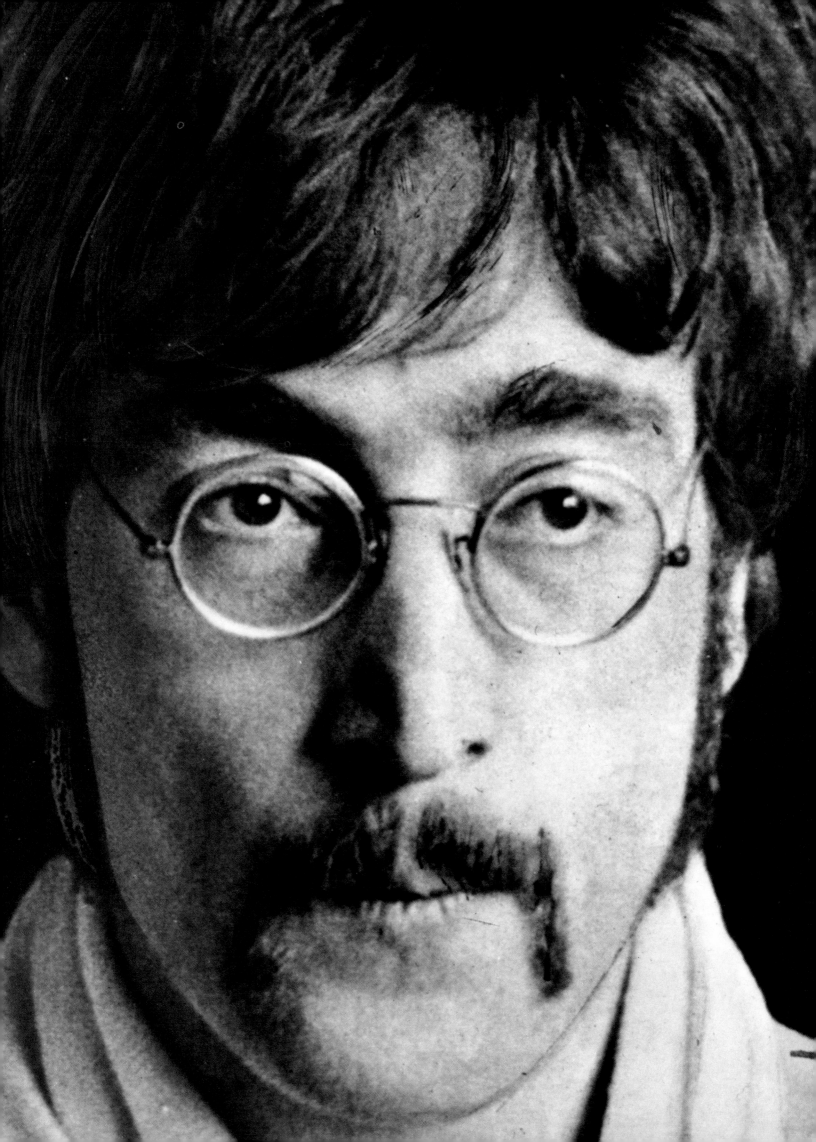

Certainly from *Revolver* on, and perhaps from *Rubber Soul*, Martin assumed a different role in the making of Beatle records. In their beginnings, he had performed sonic miracles —making them sound louder than anyone else without boosting the volume beyond normal recording levels and irritating radio stations. But by the time of *Revolver*, his job had changed. No longer did he just capture an existing sound; instead, he invented equivalents for sounds that existed only in their heads. There were times, one suspects, when he was profoundly grateful for his experience producing the old *Goon Show* records.

His more traditional musical training also came in handy during this phase of the Beatles' career, for despite their growing am-bitiousness, none could transcribe music. (George ultimately learned Eastern notation —but not your conventional "Every Good Boy Deserves Fun.") With relays of classically trained musicians popping in and out of the Beatles' recording sessions, someone had to be able to talk their language. Martin was that someone.

And, it must be said, as he brought out the best in the Beatles, so they curbed the *schlockmeister* in him. Martin had always been a skilled oboist, but as a composer (see his bits and snippets on their film tracks), he rarely rose above the musical equivalent of a fancy greeting card. On the other hand, behind both "Yesterday" and "Eleanor Rigby," his contrapuntal string arrangements balanced

Above: The 'Sgt. Pepper' days of flowered shirts, flowing capes and bushy mustaches. Paul said, "I still don't know what 'Sgt. Pepper' is all about. You meet a lot of people who think we planned all this. But we haven't, you know. We always just think of ourselves as happy little rockers playing in a rock group. But, alas, it gets more important than that after you've been over to America and get knighted and all."

the lyrics' tendency toward mawkishness. Certainly, working with the Beatles during this period, he became the first producer to build a record layer by layer—creating not a new product, but a new art.

Revolver was a prime example of the new form. In addition to—and sometimes in place of—the guitars-bass-drums lineup, the record includes brasses, strings, Indian instruments, densely multitracked vocal harmonies and, as one critic described it, "a filter that made John Lennon sound like God singing through a foghorn."

Finally, the album is significant because it made more explicit the gradually developing gulf between the group's prime composers. While Paul was elaborating the narrative techniques of "Drive My Car" into "Eleanor Rigby" and the balladeering of "Yesterday" into "Here, There and Everywhere," John was off on another trip.

Traditional doesn't seem quite the right term to use in describing speed freaks, so perhaps it's better to speak of the early Beatles as conservative. They took pills to keep going, and that was that. They didn't even begin to smoke dope until Bob Dylan turned John on after Dylan's 1964 Albert Hall concert. That event involved more than just a new substance, however, for it introduced them to a whole new *style* of drug use. The quasi-medicinal rationale that had accompanied their pill popping no longer applied; marijuana was less a prop than a consciousness-expanding recreation.

They smoked dope with the same enthusiasm they did everything else—which is to say they threw themselves headlong into the new experience. *Help!* was filmed through a haze of marijuana, and it wasn't long before they followed thousands of their peers in taking the next logical chemical step.

John and George were the first to drop acid; it was given them, curiously, by their dentist at a 1965 dinner party. But they didn't return to it for almost a year. Then, during a Los Angeles stay, John, George and Ringo began seriously taking the drug. Paul, who had still not decided to try it, felt a little out of things. Eventually, however, he came along, as did Brian, Neil Aspinall and virtually everybody else associated with the Bea-

When people want to recreate the mood of the Sixties, they will play Beatle music.

[AARON COPLAND]

tles. None, however, did it quite so thoroughly as John did.

By his own count, John had taken a thousand or so acid trips. In his famous *Lennon Remembers* interview in 1970, he said, "I used to just eat it all the time," and he doesn't seem to have been exaggerating. There were, as one might expect, consequences. Some of them were felt in his marriage—Cynthia Lennon has written that "the rot" struck them "the moment cannabis and LSD seeped its unhealthy way into our lives." The most frightening were the internal crises that overwhelmed him with a sense of worthlessness. John remembers an afternoon when publicist Derek Taylor had to talk him through one of these acid depressions. "He sort of said 'You're all right,' and pointed out which

The Beatles were enshrined at Mme. Tussaud's Wax Museum in 1964. Their images were regularly brought up to date. Here, they appear in their fifth change of clothes and hair.

Harrison

songs I had written. 'You wrote this,' and 'You said this,' and 'You are intelligent, don't be frightened.'"

But despite these surges up and down the ego ladder, John kept writing songs even during his most excessive period. Many acid-tinged works made their way onto Beatles records, and the U.K. version of *Revolver* presented a typical spectrum: "And Your Bird Can Sing," though Beatleish music, has lyrics that seem wantonly impenetrable. "Tomorrow Never Knows," however, is a still-brilliant synthesis of George's Eastern noodlings and John's inner travels; it is a period piece, perhaps, but an affecting one.

In the months after *Revolver*, in which they'd pursued their separate musical interests, they pursued separate lives as well. Three of the four were now married and Paul seemed permanently settled with acress Jane Asher. After the road and the studio, they had things to do at home.

They also had a whole world—a world that they'd helped create as the Beatles—to explore as individuals. John went off to Germany and Spain to play a small part in Richard Lester's new film, *How I Won the War*; Paul did an unimpressive film score for a Boulting Brothers comedy, *The Family Way*, which deserved even less; Ringo and Maureen vacationed in Spain, then returned to putter about their new house, and the Harrisons went to India.

While the Beatles were away, word that

Left: In August 1967, Brian died of an accidental overdose of sleeping pills. One friend said that the end of touring had made Brian "sad, almost pathetic." When George heard the news he said, "Brian's death was like the end of a chapter." Top right: Maharishi Mahesh Yogi, the Beatles' giggling guru. Bottom right: The Apple Boutique being readied to open December 1967. The 40-foot-high psychedelic mural was created by The Fool, the Dutch designers whose creations were sold in the shop. Overleaf: Studying under the Maharishi in Wales

they would no longer tour leaked out to the British press. No pop group had ever survived simply as a recording entity, so reporters pronounced the demise of the Beatles. Such was the tone taken in a lengthy London *Sunday Times* article from November 1966. "Last week," it began, "it emerged that the Beatle phenomenon was ending," and continued on to note that, "In a sense the very

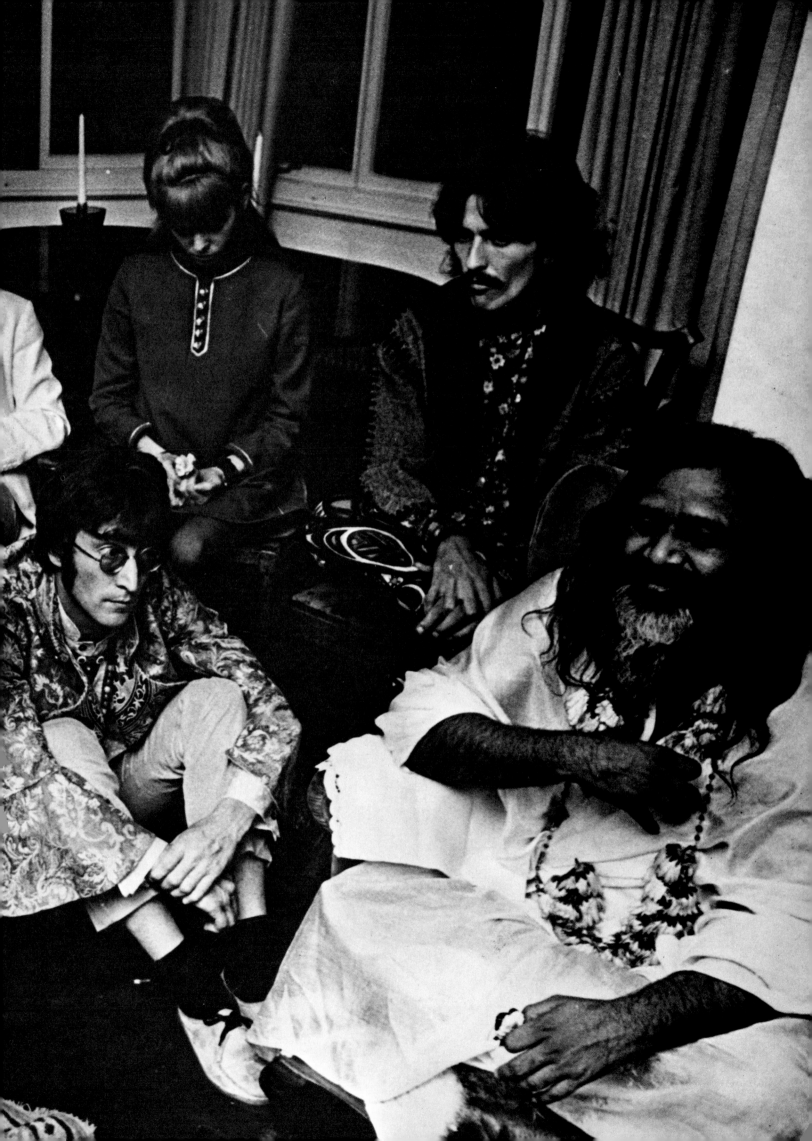

at a cost of less than $2000. *Sgt. Pepper* would take four months and cost $100,000. For today's supergroups, $100,000 barely covers the cocaine budget, but in 1967, the music business was still operating on its old assumptions. Pop groups were by definition ephemeral and the aim was to squeeze as much as possible out of them during their time in the sun. Two albums a year—one at Christmas and one for the summer—was the minimum expectation.

The Beatles had met this schedule with ease: In the two and one-half years between their first American record and *Revolver*, they had released eleven albums, tramped through thirteen major tours and made two movies. The unprecedented ten-month gap between *Revolver* and *Sgt. Pepper* had their fans waiting for a definitive breakthrough. An enticing hint of what was perhaps to be came in February 1967, with the release of the "Penny Lane"/"Strawberry Fields Forever" single.

This pair of Liverpudlian memories continued to reflect the differences between John and Paul that had surfaced during *Revolver*. But they also stretched their music further; Paul's use of trumpets in "Penny Lane," for instance, was more emotionally evocative

Ringo's mock-Tudor house in fancy Weybridge, a London suburb. The holster Elvis gave Ringo hangs in the bar. Right: Ringo in his garden of terraces and ponds, and a little woods surrounding an amphitheater. "I often think to myself," said Ringo, "What's a scruff like me doing with all this?" Overleaf: 1967

best of the Beatles' music was an expression of sheer delight at being a tightly-knit group of attractive young up-and-comers. Maturity, the waning of their collective narcissism, and the development of separate interests was bound to kill this phenomenon."

Not so fast, *Sunday Times*. Six weeks after that story appeared, the Beatles were in the studio to begin work on what many feel is their finest album, *Sgt. Pepper's Lonely Hearts Club Band.*

They had recorded their first album—a generation ago, it seemed—in a single day,

and less purely musical than the brasses in "Got to Get You into My Life." But for all its considerable charms, "Penny Lane" is painless nostalgia. By comparison, John's "Strawberry Fields" is unsettling: The virtually rhymeless lyrics circle back upon each other in a knot of self-contradiction that had fans endlessly debating their meaning.

What was perhaps most disturbing about "Strawberry Fields," however, was the affectless quality of John's vocals; it is as though he wasn't teasing us with a hidden meaning, but was hopelessly confused himself. "Strawberry Fields" is less a riddle than a mystery.

Its odd vocal timbre resulted from one of Martin's technical breakthroughs. The group

The 'Magical Mystery Tour' was conceived as "a film vehicle to go with new music," John announced. "There would be a lot of laughs, some offbeat characters, a very few glamorous girls, a bit of dancing and quite a bit of magic." It was the Beatles' first flop. Above: The bus that carried the cast and crew across Cornwall to shoot the film. Left: Beatles in white ties and tails from the movie's finale

had gotten down the basic instrumental and vocal tracks when John, listening to the tapes at home, realized the sound just wasn't what he wanted. He'd been looking for something dreamlike; this seemed too raucous, and he asked Martin to try a string arrangement. This was better, but still not perfect; what he really wanted was some of the first version *and* some of the second. Martin told him that was impossible; they'd been recorded at different tempos and in different keys. In fiddling around with the tapes, however, Martin discovered that by slowing down the first tracks, he could indeed match them to the second. The result was a slight vocal distortion that actually adds to the song's effectiveness.

Taken together, the two songs promised so much that the fans wanted more. The kids

Above: Paul, in a kitchen apron, conducting a forty-piece orchestra. Right and following pages: Shots from 'Magical Mystery Tour.' Has success spoiled the Beatles? "Well, you don't see us running around in bowler hats, do you?" said John. "I think we've pretty well succeeded in remaining ourselves."

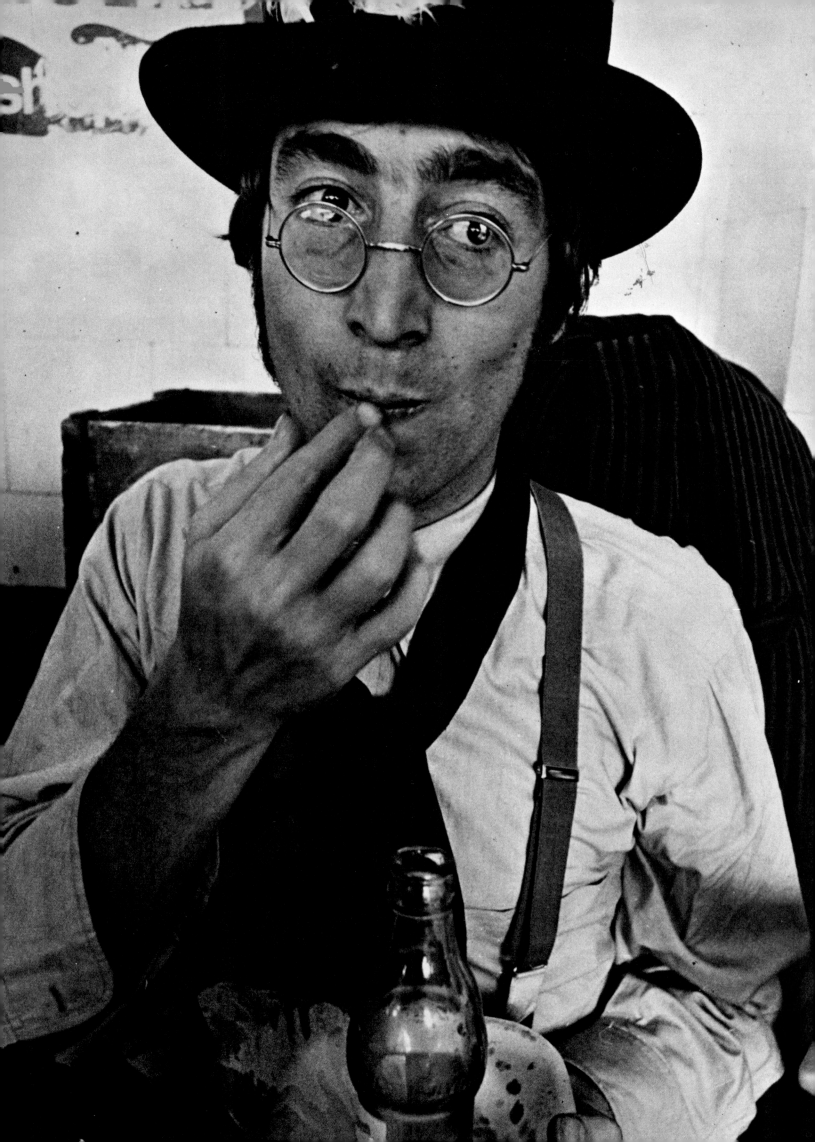

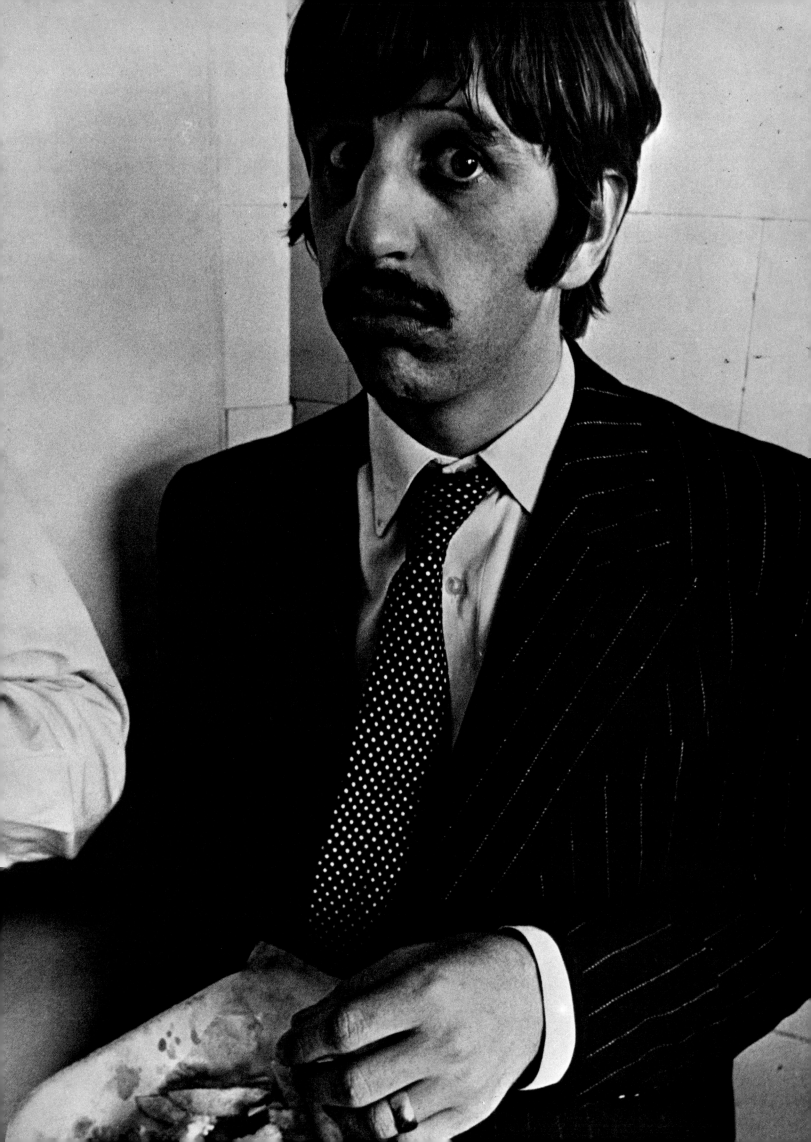

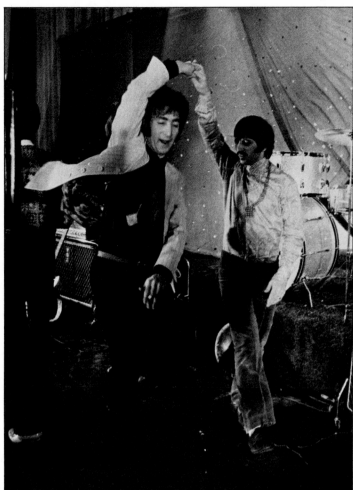

who had grown up screaming for the Beatles and the adults who'd been seduced by *A Hard Day's Night* joined to create a new kind of pop audience. There was an army of fans waiting not to dance and shriek, but to listen. Preferably stoned.

One needs to remember that the Beatles hadn't been in the vanguard of drug use, but merely a part of it. As the summer of 1967 rolled around, *everybody*, it seemed, smoked. And everybody, under the heady influence of marijuana, listened to the music exploding around them—the Airplane, the Dead, the Mamas and the Papas, Big Brother, the Who, the Stones . . . but still no Beatles.

Finally, in June—hand in hand with the much ballyhooed Summer of Love—*Sgt. Pepper* arrived. It was an amazing week. A

Left and above: The 1967 TV film 'Hello Goodbye.' "You have to be a real sour square not to love the nutty, noisy, happy, handsome Beatles," said the London 'Daily Mirror.'

year later, critic and fan (the Beatles blurred those lines) Langdon Winner recalled it: "I happened to be driving across the country on Interstate 80. In each city where I stopped for gas or food—Laramie, Oglala, Moline, South Bend—the melodies wafted in from some far-off transistor radio or portable hi-fii. It was the most amazing thing I've ever heard. For a brief while, the irreparably fragmented consciousness of the West was unified, at least in the minds of the young."

And in that magic summer, everybody was young. The hippie ghettoes in the East Village and Haight-Ashbury were overflowing with searchers after peace, love and understanding (and maybe some good acid), but they were only part of the story. On New York's West Side—and in college towns all over America—the talk was less of peace than of a war being fought halfway across the world. Peace demonstrations spread across the country, an astonishing jumble of tie-dyed jeans and seersucker suits, all in some way marching to the music the Beatles had unleashed. I am he as you are he as you are me and we are all together. Only shortly we weren't.

The illusion was valuable, however, and we rode it long enough to unhorse a president —and through some amazing textual criticism. Some fans, college-trained veterans of the New Criticism, could cheerfully follow an image down a rabbit hole and out into the forest on the other side. The forest, however, was already crowded with people who'd learned to connect images not from professors, but from smoking dope and eating acid. And so *everybody* knew about the clever trick in "*Lucy in the Sky with Diamonds.*"

We were prompted to the exegetical high

by the Beatles themselves; it was Paul, the erstwhile "cute one," who revealed their use of acid to *Life* magazine. Though Paul's confession —followed quickly by Brian's, George's and John's—was small potatoes compared to the flap over John and Jesus, there was the predictable negative reaction from the powers that be. The BBC wouldn't play "A Day in the Life," and Vice President Spiro Agnew later tried to get American radio to ban "With a Little Help from My Friends." There was an even stronger reaction from the hardcore right. Indefatigable Beatleologist Nicholas Schaffner has tracked down this splendid sample: "Neither Lennon nor McCartney were world-beaters in school," wrote a Dr. Joseph Crow, "nor have they had technical training in music. For them to have written some of their songs is like someone who had not had physics or math inventing the A-bomb. . . . Because of its technical excellence it is possible that this music is put together by behavioral scientists in some 'think tank.' . . . I have no idea whether the Beatles . . . are being used by some enormously sophisticated people, but it really doesn't make any difference. It's results that count, and the Beatles are the leading pied pipers creating promiscuity, an epidemic of drugs, youth class consciousness, and an atmosphere for social revolution." Gosh, and all along I'd thought it was George Martin.

Actually, by the time all this psychedelic whoop-de-do was going on, the Beatles had taken a hiatus from drugs to begin looking for a natural high. In this effort, at least, George was the leader. During the break between their last tour and the recording of *Sgt.*

Pepper, he and his wife, model Patti Boyd, had gone to India so that George could study with sitar virtuoso Ravi Shankar; once there, they had become fascinated by the varieties of Indian religious experience. When they returned to London, Patti joined the Spiritual Regeneration Movement, regularly passing its books and pamphlets on to George.

George had always been both open-minded (he'd been attracted by "strange" German students like Astrid) and single-minded. And just as he had bloodied his fingers learning to play the guitar, so he pursued spiritual wisdom monomaniacally. He devoured book after book, enthusiastically sharing what he'd learned with the other Beatles. He searched for his own guru as well—including one in Cornwall who kept him up on a hill for several nights—but never found one who seemed right. It was Patti who first heard that the Maharishi Mahesh Yogi was coming to give a lecture in London; she told George, and all four Beatles decided to attend.

The Maharishi had been a university-trained physicist; his own spiritual voyages had not begun until adulthood. As a result, perhaps, he was comfortable enough with the Westernized mind to find it amusing. If nothing else, the Maharishi's brand of Transcendental Meditation offered the Beatles a chance to slow down—a chance that John particularly needed.

Paul's father, who began working when he was fourteen, said "It was the happiest day of my life when Paul said I didn't need to work anymore."

The lecture captured them, as did the Maharishi's cheerful, giggling presence; from their hectic years of hermetically sealed touring, they knew too well that life was unreal. When they were offered the chance to join the Maharishi at a weekend retreat in Wales, they jumped at it. Two days later they were headed north on a British Railways train. This in itself was something of an event; they hadn't gone anywhere by public transport in years. The journey seemed an emblem of a new stage in their development.

They arrived at the retreat, endured the inevitable press conference (during which they managed to make clear that they regarded this journey as neither a lark nor a pub-

The Beatles went to India in 1968 for further meditation with their guru. John was hoping the Maharishi would save him from having to be a Beatle. But, he said, "I know he won't. He'll just tell me to go write 'Lucy in the Sky with Diamonds.'"

Are you mods or rockers? Neither. We're mockers.

[JOHN]

licity stunt), then blended in as unobtrusively as possible with the other three hundred students. It wasn't until lunchtime the next day that the reporters returned, this time carrying news: Brian Epstein was dead—a drug overdose.

They were still reacting to the shock—and still dealing with the speculation that Brian might have committed suicide—when the Maharishi called them to his private quarters. In keeping with his philosophy, he reminded them that tears and lamentations wouldn't return Brian from the dead; indeed, he said, their pain might set up vibrations that would keep Brian's spirit trapped rather than letting it rise to the next spiritual plane. They should instead be joyful, so that Brian could find joy. He comforted them, finally got them to laugh, then bade them farewell.

As the Beatles had gradually grown from teenage idols to darlings of the psychedelic intellectuals, their relationship with Brian had changed. His passionate concern with detail—a trait that had served them so well during their touring years—had come to seem an annoyance to their recording lives. There was, they felt, no need to plan ahead, no need to economize. Brian had become otiose—or even worse, a brake on what they were coming to think of as their artistic freedom.

Though the Beatles had felt liberated when they stopped touring, Brian had just felt aimless. At one point during that last San Francisco show, he had turned to a friend and asked, "What do I do now? What happens to my life?" He kept himself involved in Beatle business affairs, but somehow, it wasn't the same. Not only were their interests elsewhere; so were they. Days, even weeks, passed without him seeing or talking to them. Inevitably, the unlikely bond between them began to fray.

During a business trip to New York in the spring of 1967, for instance, Epstein was seized with a premonition of death. The Beatles were in London, laboring (and spending money) on their increasingly elaborate idea for the *Sgt. Pepper* album cover, and Brian—rather than interrupting them—wrote down his last wish and asked a friend to give it to them as soon as his plane crashed. It read: "Brown paper bags for *Sgt. Pepper*."

The wish went untransmitted, but it stands as a symbol of the growing gap between Brian and the Beatles; he had started out seeing things within them that they didn't know were there; by the time they'd reached Pepperland, they had visions of their own.

In April 1968, John and Paul (left) came to New York to announce the founding of Apple Corps. Above: At the press conference John said, "The aim of the company isn't a sack of gold teeth in the bank. It's more of a trick to see if we can get artistic freedom within a business structure."

Still, the death was a shock, and the relief that it hadn't been a suicide genuine. The "accidental" verdict allowed them to experience life without Brian free from guilt. Coupled with the Maharishi's advice, it left them feeling, in Cynthia Lennon's tellingly bland phrase, "as though [Brian] had been put on earth to do a job which was now finished."

They held a press conference to announce that they would henceforth manage themselves. John attended, but later said that when Brian died, "I knew we were in trouble then. I didn't really have any misconceptions about our ability to do anything other than play music, and I was scared. I thought, 'we've fuckin' had it.'"

In the first project the Beatles undertook without Brian (and without a George Martin equivalent), Paul took the lead. *Magical Mystery Tour* seemed a natural enough progression; as they had increasingly controlled their recordings, so they would control their films. The difference is that they had been playing music professionally for almost a decade before *Sgt. Pepper*, but had precious little experience with film. Nevertheless, within a month of Brian's death, they had embarked on their *Magical Mystery Tour*.

In the original press release announcing the film—planned as a sixty-minute TV special—John is quoted describing it as "Magicians [turning] the Most Ordinary Coach Trip into a Magical Mystery Tour," which is to say that a bus full of "ordinary" people would take what British travel agents advertise as "mystery tours"—the approximate equivalent of a shipboard "cruise to nowhere"—and have the psychedelic time of their lives.

The idea for a film about a bus tour had come to Paul in the previous April, when he was vacationing in America; though it was Paul's idea, the others were certainly enthusiastic enough about making it. But the decision to employ only the barest number of technicians and to script, direct, cast and edit the film themselves was a serious mistake. Apparently they were afraid that their unfamiliarity with the medium would let some

> ## We turned out to be a Trojan Horse. The "Fab Four" moved right to the top and then sang about drugs and sex.
> [JOHN]

"expert" take their film away from them. Not only didn't they know whom to trust, they didn't know enough to trust anyone.

But they bravely set off for two weeks of filming around Devon and Cornwall, and Paul, at least, seemed to think things had worked out all right: "For the first couple of days when we set out with this big bus full of people, we took things easy, let the ice break slowly, let everyone know what it was all about. Things just came together after that. Of course we weren't using the right jargon when we talked to the sound men and the camera crew, and they felt a bit strange to begin with. After a while, they were as enthusiastic as the rest of us."

They grew so enthusiastic, in fact, that when it came time to edit the show, the Beatles were awash in film. Paul threw himself into the task—Davies reports that though the others were present during the cutting, they were "usually having a singsong with a drunken street singer who wandered into the cutting rooms"—and emerged eleven full weeks later with the final product, just in time for the BBC Christmas season.

The critics loathed it. Indeed, since it was the first chance they'd had to slag the Beatles for anything, they seemed to get a special pleasure from their loathing—variously describing it as "appalling, naive, puffle, nonsense, contemptuous." In the wake of the onslaught, NBC canceled a million-dollar deal to show the film on American TV.

Paul, of course, was the most deeply wounded of the four, and took on the thankless burden of responding to critics, saying, "We thought the title was explanation enough. There was no plot and it was formless. Deliberately so. We enjoy fantasy and were trying to create it." Then he stubbornly announced plans to carry on: "We will make another film." Then in cheerful Beatle style he asked, "Was the film really so bad compared with the rest of the Christmas TV? You could hardly call the Queen's speech a gasser."

One suspects that there were indeed worse things on British TV that year. *Magical Mystery Tour*—especially when seen in American theaters by audiences forewarned that it was not the greatest thing since sliced bread (or even since *Help!*)—was not without its pleasures. The wonderful Busby Berkeley evocation during "Your Mother Should Know," for instance, was genuinely charming. But it's true that those moments were scattered a bit too far apart; the film lacked not mystery, but magic. Its chief importance to the Beatles

story is that it marked the emergence of Paul as the group's post-Brian leader.

One would think that *Magical Mystery Tour* had been sufficient demonstration of the perils of amateurism, but such was not the case. In a decision whose naiveté would dwarf their film-making mistakes, they decided that no men in suits were ever again going to run their lives. Brian had been all right—he was,

Ringo took this picture of himself, and Maureen with Jason (left) and Zak (right). "We called him Zak," said Ringo, "because I always wanted to be called Zak. Got it from a Western, I guess."

after all, Brian—but certainly no stranger could take his place. Besides, they were the children of the Sixties as well as its creators, and they shared the era's lively contempt for businessmen. United, they began planning to set up shop on their own.

They did so, at first, quite literally—opening their colorfully decorated Apple Boutique in London. But before they undertook the legal steps to formalize control over their fiscal empire, they paused, again in typical Sixties style, for a drop of spiritual refreshment. They left England in February on the last trip they would ever take together. Their geographical destination was Rishikesh, India, where they would continue their studies with the Maharishi.

The course was supposed to last for three months, but none of them could take it. Ringo and Maureen stayed only ten days before he announced that the whole thing reminded him of one of those fun and gamesy Butlin's resorts he used to work—and besides, the food was too spicy. Paul, who at first found the relaxed schedule conducive to songwriting, lasted a few weeks longer. When he and Jane left, however, he told reporters that the Maharishi was "a nice fellow," but "we're just not going out with him any-more."

John and George held on. They too were writing a lot of music—most of which would make its way onto *The White Album*—and the meditation did seem to be providing the spiritual, or at least emotional, rewards they were seeking. But accurately or not, they became convinced that the Maharishi had distinctly worldly designs on one of their illustrious fellow students, actress Mia Farrow. They confronted him, in an oblique way, with this accusation, and when he was unable to answer it, or even figure out precisely what it was, they headed back to London. There John announced that the Maharishi's method was nothing but a lot of "colored water," and composed "Sexy Sadie" in the guru's (dis)honor.

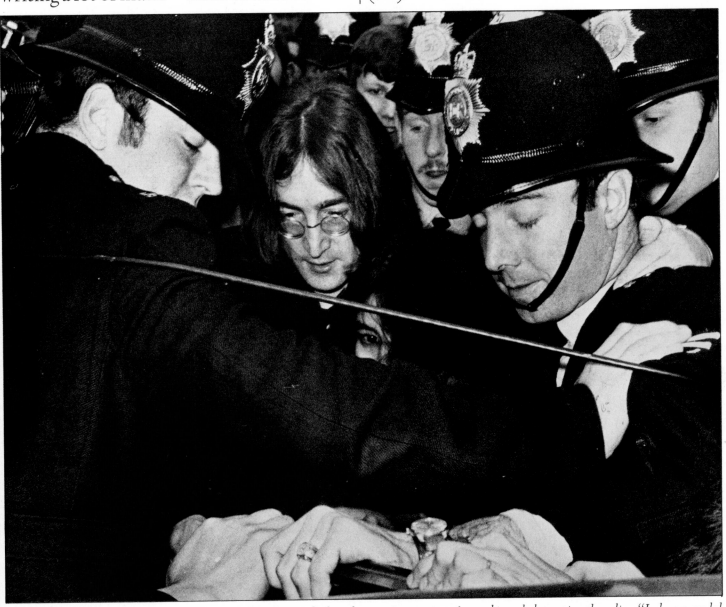

October 1968. A noontime bust at John and Yoko's flat resulted in charges of possession of cannabis and obstructing the police. "I always needed a drug to survive," said John. "The others did too, but I always had more."

But George felt the experience differently. Though disappointed in the Maharishi personally, he felt that the Eastern way contained a central truth that was still worth seeking. One problem, he thought, was that the Maharishi's discipline was too easy, and in London, George submitted himself to the more rigorous programs of Krishna Consciousness. Without any deliberate intent, he was taking the first step toward breaking up the Beatles.

Until then, there had been—for each of them—nothing more important than the other three. But when George began following his own path toward enlightenment, he left his mates behind. The "actual world," he told Davies, "is an illusion. It's been created by worldly minds. It doesn't matter what happens, the plan can't be affected, even having wars or dropping an H-bomb; none of it matters. It's only what happens in ourselves which matters."

One thing that did matter to George was happening rather more within himself than he wished. In the time since they'd stopped touring, he had begun to rival John and Paul as a songwriter—at least in terms of quantity. Yet they still got more space on albums, and he complained bitterly to a friend that only one of his songs had ever been released as a single—and that one, "The Inner Light," as a very definite B-side to "Lady Madonna."

While George was imbibing his heady brew of suppressed anger and Krishna cool, the Beatles' business plans progressed. John and Paul traveled to America in the early summer of 1968 to celebrate the formation of the Beatles' latest interest: Apple Corps, Ltd. Seated on a Chinese junk in the Hudson River, Paul proclaimed Apple a sort of "Western Communism," the corporate vehicle by which the Beatles would not only manage their own lives, but bring joy to the lives of others as well. The aim, John explained, was to see "if we can get artistic freedom within a business structure, to see if we can create things and sell them without charging three times our cost." In a final coda, Paul pointed out that the Beatles were "in the happy position of not needing any more money, so for the first time the bosses aren't in it for the profit. If you come and see me and say, 'I've had such-and-such a dream,' I will say, 'Here's so much money. Go away and do it.'"

The extraordinary thing is less that there were hundreds of hopeful dreamers who believed this promise than that the Beatles appeared to believe it themselves; their Liverpool street smarts had been psychedelicized and lionized plum out of them. And as though these press conferences weren't lure enough, they actually paid for advertisements in the British music weeklies urging "undiscovered" musicians to send their tapes to "Apple Music, 94 Baker St., London W.1."

Western Communism dealt with the resultant sea of tapes by efficiently, if unimaginatively, neglecting to listen to most of them. Live petitioners were more difficult. Derek Taylor, who returned to the Beatles after Brian's death to serve as Apple's publicist, has recounted his acid-tinged memories of those days in his memoir. Among the all-too-typical visitors he recalled was one Hugh Blackwell, who wanted £50,000 "because he is now *all* of the people mentioned in both

---

Following pages: John, Paul, George and Ringo, photographed by Richard Avedon, January 1968

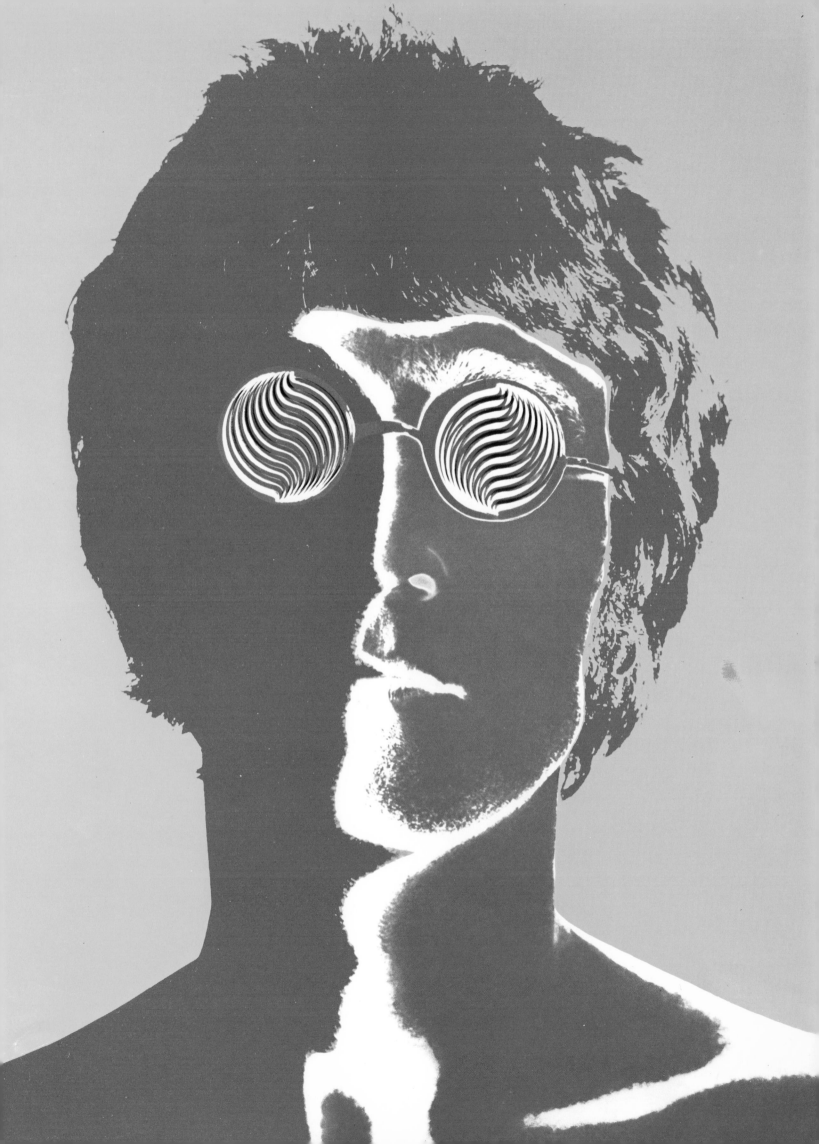

Sgt. Pepper's Lonely Hearts Club Band and in *John Wesley Harding* and in addition he is Popeye the Sailor Man and he needs every penny he can get to act out this amalgam in a movie."

The Hugh Blackwells of the world could, like the tapes, simply not be listened to, but others—particularly old friends and acquaintances—did receive help. Some received more than the Beatles had planned and cash virtually streamed from the organization—especially out of the Apple Boutique.

In July, the Beatles finally ran out of patience and ordered it closed. (This, at least, was handled with style; the merchandise was simply given away to whoever wandered into the store.)

Characteristically, it was Paul who told Apple's staff what was going on. By then, the other Beatles were losing interest and Paul was left to putter around the office and see that there was enough toilet paper in the lavatories. His presence alone, however, was not enough to stem the steady hemorrhaging of cash, and by the time Apple's first year-end results were audited (naturally, this didn't occur until 1970), the accountants were forced to write off no fewer than three automobiles because they could find neither receipts for their purchase nor, alas, the cars themselves.

After the *Magical Mystery Tour* debacle, the chance of the Beatles once again directing themselves in a feature film (and getting distribution for it) varied between slim and none. But they owed United Artists one more film under the contract that had provided *Help!* and *A Hard Day's Night*. Before he died, Brian fortunately had found a way around this obligation by arranging to have "the Beatles" star in a cartoon feature. Al Brodax, an American who had produced half-hour Saturday-morning Beatles cartoons for ABC-TV, was brought in to produce *Yellow Submarine*. When they saw the final product, the Beatles themselves were so delighted that they agreed to play in the film's closing sequence.

This turned out to be something of a mixed blessing—Brodax recalls Ringo one day showing up at the studio so stoned he could do nothing but walk around in circles until he eventually calmed himself down by tripping over a glockenspiel and passing out —but when the film was released in the summer of 1968, it turned out to be a tasty confection. None of the critics confused it with great art, but even the most skeptical were disarmed by its easy amusements. The most interesting reaction, however, came from *The New York Times*, where film reviewer Renata Adler ever so discreetly suggested that her readers might wish to get stoned. She argued that *Yellow Submarine*'s particular virtue—a "sense of perception washed clean"—was "certainly accessible to people who are not high, but in an overstimulated urban environment, probably rarely. There is certainly no point in seeing *Yellow Submarine*, or anything else that is good, drunk. But the best music has been most accessible to an occasional high for a long time, and movies, as it turns out more and more, are such an intensely musical form—well, the audiences at *Yellow Submarine* so far have been largely, not stupid and blunted like three-martini audiences, but fresh and open and precise in their response."

As their cartoon surrogates fought off the Blue Meanies, the Beatles themselves were back in the studio; their first product on their new label was a stunner—the double-sided hit single of "Hey Jude"/"Revolution." "Jude" reflects Paul's painful breakup with Jane Asher. In addition to being one of the rare ballads where McCartney wrestles directly with emotions rather than sentimentalizing them, "Jude" cracked AM radio's rigid format like a matchstick; clocked at 7:11, it still stands as the longest number-one single ever.

In that sense, at least, the Apple experiment looked as though it might work; it had given the Beatles a chance to break the rules of pop programing, and because they were the Beatles, they got away with it handsomely. Still, the recording sessions for their first Apple album—formally titled *The Beatles* but universally referred to as *The White Album*—

'Yellow Submarine,' a full-length animated cartoon, had only four new songs in it. Above: Paul, Ringo and George pose with a cutout of John to promote the movie. Right: John took this picture when he was shooting the cover of 'Two Virgins,' the album he made with Yoko in 1968. The newspaper did not show up on the album cover photo. "Some people think they're mad," said Ringo, "but he's only being John."

were anything but smooth. They produced, in fact, the first Beatles breakup.

Oddly, it was quiet Ringo who walked out the door. One of his reasons for going might have been, as Hunter Davies suggests, that the end of touring was harder on him than on anyone else. Paul and John were always involved up to their ears in the technical side of their recordings, and George—though he had to fight with Paul for album space—was always in charge of recording his own compositions. Live, Ringo had been the fourth Beatle, but in the studio, he was a fifth wheel, endlessly hanging about and waiting for the next take in which—as the Beatles arrangements became more complicated and baroque—his drums played a steadily less prominent role. Some frustration was therefore inevitable, but friends of Ringo's say it was heightened by Paul's relentless criticisms of Ringo's technique—and capped when Paul suggested that he himself should take over the drums on his own songs.

The split lasted for only a week, however, and Ringo returned, uttering oblique phrases about "musical disagreements," and noting that "Paul is the greatest bass guitar player in the world. But he is also very determined; he goes on and on to see if he can get his own way." When Ringo returned, he found that Paul had welcomed him back by decking his drums with flowers.

He also found that Yoko Ono, feeling fluish, had moved her bed into the studio.

Yoko—an ambitious conceptual artist who was always clever, sometimes brilliant and usually abrasive—was like nothing the Beatles had ever seen before. Jane Asher had maintained a certain independence during

her long liaison with Paul, but the Beatles' wives were decidedly domestic. Beatles groupies—the other women in their lives—were as disposable as Kleenex. Yoko was something else.

John had first met her during her one-woman show at London's Indica Gallery in late 1966. He was fascinated—first by her work, and then by her. They became friends, beginning a long-distance correspondence that lasted through her stays in America and his Indian trip. Eventually, in a reversal of usual Beatle behavior, he fell mind-first in love with her.

Tittenhurst Park, the Georgian mansion acquired by John and Yoko in 1969. Paul said, "At the beginning of their relationship, I was annoyed at John, jealous of Yoko, and afraid about the breaking of a great musical partnership. It took me a year to realize they were in love."

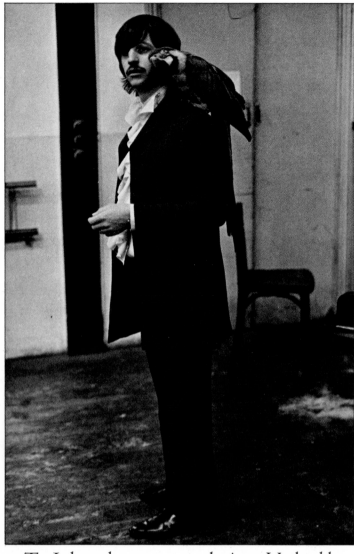

To John, she was a revelation. He had begun to detect the glimmerings of a new cause when he read about the women's movement. In Yoko, who was able and eager to spar with him intellectually, he found the movement personified. "I don't know how it happened," he has said, "I just realized that she knew everything I knew—and more, probably—and that it was coming out of a woman's head, it just sort of bowled me over. It was like finding gold or something. . . . As she was talking to me I would get high, and the discussion would get to such a level that I would be goin' higher and higher. When she'd leave I'd go back to this sort of suburbia. Then I'd meet her again, and me head

"We can't go on holding hands forever," said John. "The Beatles— those four jolly lads. But we're not those people anymore. We're old men. We still enjoy it, but sometimes we feel silly."

would go open like I was on an acid trip.'' In a way that seems funny, considering the Beatles' sexual adventurism, she shocked the boys' sensibilities profoundly.

She and John became lovers, after a two-year celibate courtship, in Lennon's suburban house. His marriage to Cynthia had become increasingly strained. She was once again away in Spain and, as he told *Rolling Stone*, ''I thought now's the time if I'm ever gonna get to know [Yoko] anymore. She came to the house, and I didn't know what to do; so we went upstairs to my studio and I played her all the tapes that I'd made, all this far-out stuff, some comedy stuff and some electronic music. She was suitably impressed and then she said, 'Let's make one ourselves,' so we made *Two Virgins*. It was midnight when we started *Two Virgins*, it was dawn when we finished, and then we made love at dawn. It was very beautiful.''

They found it so beautiful, indeed, that they could hardly wait to tell the world about it; they did so by releasing *Two Virgins* in November 1968—the same month as *The White Album*. *Two Virgins* was remarkable for its music—two sides of seemingly random bird calls, screeches and nose-blowings—but notorious for its cover. There, arms around each other and naked, stood the two lovers. And there, unambiguously, was a Beatle cock.

EMI refused to distribute the album. Other companies agreed to try, but covering it with a plain brown wrapper didn't help; thousands of copies were confiscated as obscene. This was not lovable moptopdom, and many of the Beatles' younger fans—along with virtually all their parents—echoed the sentiments of a hastily recorded single called ''John, You Went Too Far This Time.'' Paul's comment was both more poignant and less commercially inspired: ''John's in love with Yoko, and he's no longer in love with the three of us.''

Nevertheless, all the Beatles—except John, apparently—found *Two Virgins* more tolerable than the notion of Yoko as the fifth Beatle. Though she was arrogantly sure of her genius, she was a square peg in no hole as far

Earlier, Paul had said, "This rumor that we're splitting is rubbish. We're all great friends and we don't want to split up." But by now, signs of alienation were beginning to show.

as the Beatles were concerned. They didn't particularly like her at a distance; as a constant comrade following John into the men's room so they could continue their conversations, they found her unbearable. And when he tried to impose her musical suggestions on their work, they found her a threat.

Jilted by both Jane and John, Paul did not stay long alone. After a brief fling with Francie Schwartz (who bounced from his bed to the typewriter with unseemly haste), he hooked up with Linda Eastman. She had come from the same suburban town as Yoko—Scarsdale, where her high school yearbook records her as having "a yen for men"—but their careers could not have been more divergent. Yoko, whether a good one or a bad, was an artist; Linda, though a sometime photographer, was best known as a groupie.

But she was, it seems, exactly what Paul needed—or at least wanted. She was the extreme example of the man-identified woman, and Hunter Davies has shrewdly speculated that this was perhaps her chief attraction: "I'd always presumed that an adoring fan would be the last thing he would want, having been pursued by them for so long. What I hadn't realized was that, in his enclosed life with John, whose cynicism and brutal honesty kept Paul on his toes, and with Jane Asher, who was as strong in her opinions as Paul, he could quite possibly have felt cramped and constrained. . . . Linda came along at the right time for Paul (just as John was moving off) and encouraged Paul not to feel inferior, to be his own man—he could do anything if he tried."

Thus John and Paul, each in his own way, offered in their comparative maturity a testimony to the belief that had informed virtually all their early songwriting and recording—the primacy of romantic love. Living out the myth was harder, however, for romance bumped up against an equally compelling myth—the Beatles. Seen in this context, Paul's remark about John loving Yoko is a painfully correct analysis of the problem that confronted the Beatles as it would confront their peers: the conflict between the existence of couples and the demands of cooperative group activity. The pain of the Beatles' breakup is proof of just how deeply they believed in both sides of the equation.

The White Album was released, with its typical quota of two Harrison songs per record, and promptly went to number one. But as John would later say, "There isn't any Beatle music on it. . . . It was John and the Band, Paul and the Band, George and the Band, like that."

Shortly after *The White Album* topped the charts, John offhandedly told a newspaper reporter that "Apple is losing money. If it carries on like this, we'll be broke in six months." This was an exaggeration, of course, but it provoked a transatlantic phone call to John from Allen Klein. Klein, a tough-talking streetwise New York accountant who had made a brilliant career extracting money from record companies on behalf of such clients as the Rolling Stones, said he'd certainly like to come over and help straighten Apple out.

He was not the only one with such ideas, however, nor even the first. Paul's father-in-law-to-be, Lee Eastman, was a leading international copyright lawyer; even his enemies, of whom he had many, agreed that he was perhaps the most outstanding technician in his field. Together with his son John, he had developed Eastman and Eastman into one of New York's most successful specialized law firms. Over dinner at Eastman's home, Paul mentioned his frustrations with Apple. Eastman said he would be delighted to help and promptly dispatched his son to London.

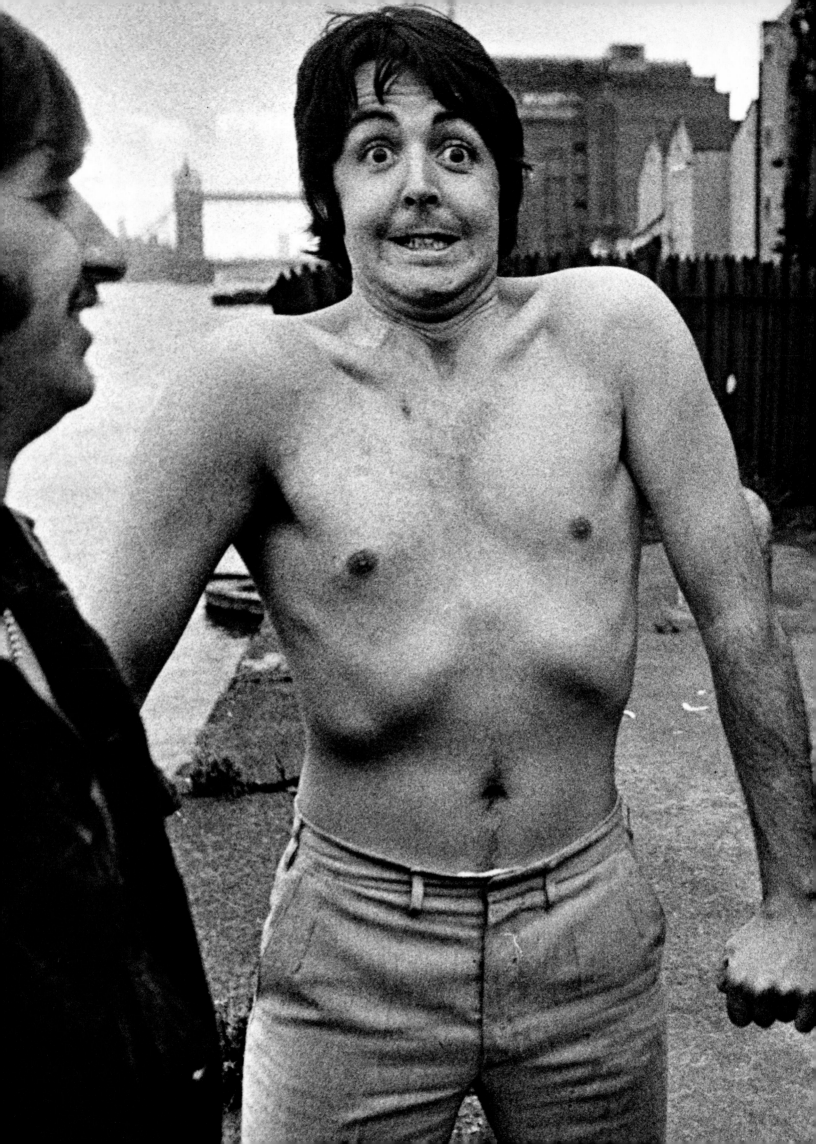

John Eastman did not claim to know much about pop music, but he recognized that Brian Epstein's death had left the Beatles in a troubled fiscal position. Brian's management firm, Nems, continued to exist—now managed by Brian's brother Clive, who wanted more than anything else to return to the furniture business. It also continued to take twenty-five percent off the top of the Beatles' earnings. Even more seriously, the closely held company was going to be severely hit by the estate taxes attendant on Brian's death. Eastman's solution was elegantly simple: The Beatles should arrange a loan (in the form of a royalty advance from EMI) and use it to buy Nems themselves. For a million pounds they could not only recapture the twenty-five percent, they could also shift their tax liability into a more manageable capital-gains category. He explained the situation to the Beatles, and they agreed to follow his advice;

In the late years of the Beatles, group photo sessions became increasingly rare. The photos, carefully produced and released by the Apple office, were used to promote their records. These pictures date from 'The Beatles' ('The White Album').

Can't have a party
without Beatles records...
[ERIC BURDON]

they also—all of them—agreed to appoint him Apple's general counsel. Clive Epstein had already accepted Eastman's offer by the time Klein arrived in London.

Klein met first with John and Yoko. During a lengthy session at the Dorchester Hotel, he talked hardly at all about money; instead, he talked about the Beatles—their music and their position in the pop world. By the time John left, he was convinced that Allen Klein would be the answer to all their problems. When Linda Eastman heard the news, her first comment was, "Oh, shit."

Paul directing the ill-fated recording session of the "roots" album 'Let It Be.' Right: Ringo taking a break. Above: Yoko sits between John and Paul. "I can't forgive Paul and George for the way they treated Yoko at first. But I can't help loving them, either," John (top) said.

The greatest composers since Beethoven.

[LONDON SUNDAY TIMES]

Though their management advice might often overlap, Klein and the Eastmans represented radically different styles. Lee Eastman had Anglicized his name (from Epstein, as it happens) when he graduated from Harvard Law School; Klein remained active in the Jewish community. Eastman summered in the Hamptons; Klein liked Miami and Las Vegas. John and George and Ringo liked Klein; Paul loved Linda.

Paul had left the first meeting with Klein early, but at the second—which John Eastman also attended—Paul took the questions Klein raised about the Nems purchase seri-

The Beatles gave a lunchtime concert on Apple's rooftop to the crowd in the street below until an irate banker protested to the police.

ously. Since the million-pound "loan" from EMI was actually an advance on salary, Klein pointed out, it was taxable; that meant they might not be able to afford a million-pound purchase. Or, he added, they might. It depended on what their full royalty was to be and what their other liabilities were. He thought the deal should be delayed until he'd had the chance to examine their full financial picture. The Beatles and Eastman all agreed with him, and on that same afternoon, Klein met with Clive Epstein and was assured that Nems would go along with a three-week postponement of the purchase. Two weeks later, however, Epstein sold Nems to an investment trust—because, he said, of a letter he had received from Apple counsel John Eastman. Later, he described John Eastman as "a little too young to be negotiating at that level."

Even as corporate sharks tore at chunks of their fortunes, the Beatles struggled to make music. They were at Twickenham Film Studios to record an album of "roots" music, the basic rock 'n' roll that had inspired them a decade earlier. To the normal tensions of recording—and the abnormal strain of their fiscal frolics—they added yet a third aggravation: the steady, whirring presence of cameras filming a documentary of the fabulous Beatles making a record.

It wasn't so fabulous. About a week after filming began, George became the second Beatle to leave the band. He had come back to England, from a brief American tour with Eric Clapton, full of self-confidence and overflowing with new songs he'd written. He rapidly discovered that Paul was not impressed: "This cooperation [in America] contrasted dramatically with the superior atti-

When Paul and Linda Eastman (left) were married in London in March 1969, the bride said to the press, "Be sure to say I was wearing a big smile." Above: Mr. Allen Klein, the Beatles' last money manager.

tude which for years Paul had shown to me musically," he later said. "In normal circumstances, I had let him have his own way, even when this meant that songs which I had composed were not being recorded. . . . I was in a very happy frame of mind, but I quickly discovered I was up against the same old Paul. . . . In front of the cameras, as we were actually being filmed, Paul started to 'get at' me about the way I was playing."

Paul had indeed done that, but not necessarily from a sense of superiority. If anything, it was more like desperation. In the absence of Brian, and with John totally monopolized by Yoko, Paul either had to face the end of the Beatles or struggle to keep them going himself. He carried the burden with as much grace as possible, as indicated by this bit of tape-recorded dialogue from the studio:

Paul: "I mean we've been very negative since Mr. Epstein passed away . . . That's why all of us in turn have been sick of the group, you know. It is a bit of a drag. It's like when you're growing up—your daddy goes away at a certain point in your life and then you stand on your own feet. Daddy has gone away now, you know. I think we either go home, or we do it.

"It's discipline we need. Mr. Epstein, he said, 'Get suits on' and we did. And so we were always fighting that discipline a bit. But now it's silly to fight that discipline if it's our own. It's self-imposed these days, so we do as little as possible. But I think we need a bit more if we are going to get on with it."

George: "Well, if that's what doing it is, I don't want to do anything."

Nobody, it seemed, really did. Ringo and Paul stood virtually alone as keepers of the Beatle flame. And because the band was trying for a "live" feeling, the tensions grew steadily worse; each time one of them would fluff a note or miss a beat, all four had to start the song over again. And over.

Finally, for the first time in their career, they gave up and went home, leaving the film, the book, the songs—and perhaps the Beatles—behind them.

On March 12th, Paul and Linda were married. (George and Patti were busted for drugs that day, by the same officer who'd busted John and Yoko the preceding fall.) They escaped the crowd gathered outside the Marylebone Registry office and vanished into seclusion. Eight days later, on Gibraltar, John and Yoko wed in an even quieter ceremony. They did not go into seclusion.

Upper left: John and Yoko return from their wedding in Gibraltar. "It was perfect. Quick, quiet and British," said John. Right: John and Yoko's Christmas message. "I really thought love would save us all." Overleaf: A last group shot, 1969

WAR
IS OVER!
IF YOU WANT IT
Happy Christmas from John & Yoko
CAR
PARK
ENTER FROM DENMAN ST.
TYRANT KING
Hyde Park Corner
Piccadilly Bloomsbury
Islington Dalston
Clapton Lea Bridge Rd
38
CLAPTON
VERNONS
£345,160
COURT TEXTILES

THE NEW YORK TIMES, SATURDAY, APRIL 11, 1970

McCartney Breaks Off With Beatles

By ALVIN SHUSTER
Special to The New York Times

LONDON, April 10—Paul McCartney said today he had broken with the Beatles over a series of differences.

The announcement could mean the end of future recordings by the world's most successful pop group, which started 10 years ago in a cellar in Liverpool, became a social phenomenon in the 1960's, influenced the hair styles and musical tastes of millions and placed an indelible mark on the history of show business.

Mr. McCartney, who composed the Beatle songs in partnership with John Lennon, another member of the group, said the break was the result of "personal differences, business differences, musical differences—but most of all because I have a better time with my family."

In a statement taking the form of an interview with himself, Mr. McCartney said he no longer wanted to record with the group nor write any more songs with Mr. Lennon. But he qualified this by saying he did not know whether the break was temporary or permanent.

There have long been rumors that the Beatles were breaking up as a combo to let their talents evolve in different direc-

Associated Press
Paul McCartney

tions. Their last "live" appearance was during their 1966 tour of the United States. Since then Ringo Starr and George Harrison have made solo records, Mr. Lennon and his wife, Yoko Ono, have formed the Plastic Ono Band, and Mr. McCartney has just completed a long-playing record of his own.

The last group album appeared in August, 1969, and the four have one more due out at the end of this month. Spokesmen at the Beatles office agreed it could be the last joint effort for some time.

Derek Taylor, the spokesman for Apple Corps, Ltd., the Beatles' omnibus business group for film, electronics and other ventures, said that because of the McCartney statement the Beatles "could be dormant for years." He added that "it is certain that at the moment they could not comfortably work together."

A chief reason for the decision by Mr. McCartney seems to be differences with his colleagues over the appointment last year of Allen Klein, a flamboyant, 35-year-old American, as the financial adviser to the Beatles. Mr. McCartney, who is 27 years old, reportedly wanted his father-in-law, Lee Eastman of New York, to replace him.

In his statement, Mr. McCartney reflected his unhappiness with Mr. Klein, saying that "I am not in contact with him and he does not represent me in any way."

There have also been reports in pop-music publications of a growing rift between Mr. McCartney and Mr. Lennon. Some stories suggested that Mr. McCartney and the other Beatles were unhappy over the growing influence of Mr. Lennon's wife, and were unwilling to admit a fifth Beatle.

NEW YORK POST, MONDAY, APRIL 13, 1970

When Yoko Walked In, McCartney Said 'O No!'

By DAVID LANCASHIRE

LONDON (AP)—The official biographer of the Beatles says the major cause of the breakup of the pop quartet appeared to be John Lennon's marriage to Yoko Ono.

"If there was one single element in the split, I'd say it was the arrival of Yoko," said Hunter Davies, author of "The Beatles, An Official Biography."

While he was writing the book, Davies was the most intimate confidant of the Beatles outside their own music and business organization.

Writing in the Sunday Times, Davies said that after Lennon and Yoko got together "the rest of the Beatles didn't matter any more." Lennon and Yoko were married in Gibraltar in March last year.

Long-rumored differences among the Beatles came out in the open in a statement from Paul McCartney saying he was splitting from the group—and "time will tell" whether temporarily or permanently.

Davies said that since the Beatles hadn't performed together in person since 1966, McCartney's statement "was pretty pointless."

McCartney himself, in an interview with Raymond Palmer in the News of the World, said: "No matter how much we split, we're still very linked. We're the only four people who've seen the whole Beatlemania bit

from the inside out, so we're tied forever, whatever happens."

McCartney did not clarify in detail his reasons for breaking away from the group.

But Davies maintained that under Yoko's influence, Lennon began taking charge at Apple, the Beatles' business headquarters, and this "was a blow to Paul's pride . . . Paul fell by the wayside and . . . they were no longer bosom buddies . . . George Harrison and Ringo Starr [the other two Beatles] are not exactly dotty over or endeared to Yoko either."

With Yoko, Lennon has mounted campaigns for world peace, held zany art exhibitions, made radical movies, formed a wild rock and roll band and issued non-Beatle records. None of these activities included the other Beatles.

So far Lennon, Harrison and Ringo have kept silent about McCartney's breakaway. McCartney himself didn't make his reasons much clearer than his original vague announcement.

Asked by Palmer what sort of things he might try on his own, McCartney replied: "Anything and everything. There's no point in restricting yourself . . .

"After you've gone through the whole bit of performing and showing everyone how famous you are, you realize that you don't need to show anyone any more."

Beatles in Court Battle Call Paul 'Spoiled Child'

LONDON (UPI) — Ringo Starr, George Harrison and John Lennon described fellow Beatle Paul McCartney yesterday as a spoiled child who tried to teach them how to play their own instruments. But they fought back against McCartney's efforts to name a receiver for the group.

McCartney appeared before the British High Court of Justice last week to challenge Allen Klein's position as manager for the group and to charge their finances were in precarious shape. He asked that a receiver succeed Klein.

Yesterday the other three Beatles presented statements through their lawyers supporting Klein and detailing their difficulties with McCartney during their rise to fame and fortune. Ringo told the court yesterday he thought the four men could work out everything satisfactorily.

Lennon started things off today with a written statement saying the Beatles' Apple Company was "full of hustlers and spongers" after the death of their original manager, Brian Epstein. He said when Klein took control in early 1969 he dismissed incompetent and unnecessary staff and the "hustling and lavish spending" ended at the Apple offices.

Harrison told the high court he had to put up with McCartney "telling me how to play my own musical instrument" and that McCartney "started to get at me" while cameras were turning for the film "Let It Be" and that he decided he had had enough.

"I had always let him have his own way, even when this meant that songs which I had composed were not being recorded," Harrison's statement said.

"At the same time I was helping to record his songs and into the bargain I was having to put up with him telling me how to play my own musical instrument."

Ringo told the court McCartney behaved "like a spoiled child" and that when the Apple company decided to delay release of McCartney's solo album "McCartney" because of Ringo's solo album "Sentimental Journeys" he went to see Paul.

"To my dismay, he went completely out of control, shouting at me, prodding his fingers toward my face and saying 'I'll finish you now' and 'you'll pay,'" the Starr statement said.

"He told me to put my coat on and get out," said Ringo, whose real name is Richard Starkey. "I did so."

Lawsuit Spells Breakup for Beatles

From left: Ringo Starr, John Lennon, Paul McCartney and George Harrison at a ceremony in 1965

Associated Press

McCartney Splits With The Beatles

LONDON (AP)—Paul McCartney announced today that he's split from the Beatles—but said he may be back.

This first open rift in the world's top pop group was announced from Apple, the company which manages Beatle affairs.

Paul, 27-year-old song-writer, lead guitar and singer, blamed the break on "personal differences, business differences, musical differences—but most of all because I have a better time with my family."

McCartney is married to an American, Linda Eastman of New York. They have a 7-month-old daughter, Mary, and Linda has another daughter, Heather, by an earlier marriage.

No More Together?

McCartney's statement, issued alongside his first solo album, said he does not know whether the rift is permanent or temporary.

The Beatles as a group have one more LP in the can for release next month. It is doubtful whether they will ever record together again.

Officials at Apple have long resisted any suggestion that Beatledom had reached its end. Then Mavis Smith, the company's spokesman, mitted to day th been month nev

JOHN LENNON
Bye, bye, Paul.

He sa

By ANTHONY LEWIS
Special to The New York Times

LONDON, Dec. 31 — The Beatles, collective folk heroes of the nineteen-sixties, finally broke apart today.

Paul McCartney brought suit in the High Court here to end the partnership. He named as defendants the other members of the pop group: John Lennon, George Harrison and Ringo Starr.

The writ claimed that their relationship as "The Beatles and Company" should "be dissolved." It asked for an accounting of assets and income, still thought to be running to $17 - million a year.

For many months there has been talk of a final Beatle bust - up. The four have long since given up personal appearances together.

They did release a record, "Let It Be," last May, and a movie of the same name followed, but they have increasingly operated as individuals.

The legal conflict that began today makes it unlikely that the Beatles will again perform as an entity. In a way, the fact that one of the four should go to law against the others symbolized the end of an innocent pop age.

When the Beatles first emerged from Liverpool to world fame, in 1963, they had longish hair and funny, round haircuts. Their faces and their manner had a winning innocence that enhanced their genuinely fresh musical style.

Now all four have beards, and all have married. They have lost the teen-age look —their ages range from 28 to 30. They have been involved in political protest and mysticism and business.

Mr. Lennon and Mr. McCartney wrote the songs for of the four, or at least the most creative musically. He has played a leading part, along with the Beatles' arranger and recording manager, George Martin, in the often novel instrumentation and chords.

Early in 1970, Mr. McCartney was interviewed by a London expert on the pop-world, Ray Connolly. He said then: "The Beatles have left the Beatles—but no one wants to say the party's over. John's in love with Yoko, and he's no longer in love with the other three of us."

Mr. Lennon, for his part, said in an interview in the magazine, Rolling Stone, that Mr. McCartney was to blame. He accused Mr. McCartney of trying to "take over" after the death of their manager, Brian Epstein, in 1967.

Mr. Epstein was widely considered the moving force that made the Beatle phenomenon possible, in terms of both publicity and finance. At his death many predicted a break-up, and they turned out to be right.

Last March Mr. McCartney brought out a record album of his own, a symptom of change in the relationship. The others have also tried to the Beatles, and they were always regarded as closest to each other personally. They first met at a village fair outside Liverpool 14 years ago.

But Mr. Lennon has gone off on his own in recent years. With his Japanese wife, Yoko Ono, he has made a splash with nudity on record sleeves, with public "bed-ins" and with campaigns against the Vietnam war.

The musical world has tended to regard Mr. McCartney as the most gifted stake themselves out as independent personalities.

They went instead to the Amsterdam Hilton, issuing a press release inviting reporters to a "happening" that was to take place in their bed. Imagining the obvious, and suspecting the worst, the Amsterdam police issued a statement warning that, "If people are invited to such a 'happening,' the police will certainly act."

In retrospect, one sort of wishes they had, for all John and Yoko did was announce that they planned to stay in bed for a week and grow their hair for peace, as "a protest against all the suffering and violence in the world." During their honeymoon they also introduced "bagism" at an Austrian press conference conducted from within a sack, planted acorns "for peace" in front of an English cathedral, and bedded down in Canada.

In the midst of all this, John somehow found time to compose "The Ballad of John and Yoko," which he wanted very much to release as a Beatles single. Since there is a case to be made that John's love for Yoko effectively ended the Beatles, there was no little irony in his desire. At first, it seemed impossible to realize; Ringo was on location filming *The Magic Christian*, and George, perhaps strategically, was also unavailable. But Paul knew what love meant—he loved Linda, after all, *and* John—so he obligingly overdubbed the drums while John took both guitar parts. John returned the gesture when "Give Peace a Chance," which he recorded with the Plastic Ono Band, was credited to "Lennon/McCartney."

The various honeymoons came to an abrupt end, however, when Dick James, the dynamic duo's long-time publisher, announced that he was selling Northern Songs, which held the rights to all Lennon/McCartney compositions, to an entertainment conglomerate headed by Sir Lew Grade. During the Canada bed-in, John was asked a question about the sale and rapidly put aside the talk of peace to reveal his fighting side. "I won't sell," he said. "They are my shares and my songs and I want to keep a bit of the end product. I don't have to ring Paul; I know damn well he feels the same as I do."

We were just a band who made it very big. That's all.
[JOHN]

John was right. In this battle, at least, he and Paul were as one. They settled in for a lengthy proxy fight that even briefly put Klein and the Eastmans on the same track. Klein was also busy with other Beatle business. He renegotiated the band's contract with EMI—achieving the highest royalty rate in the history of the industry—and eventually put together a settlement ending Nems' control of the Beatles' earnings. Despite his continuing alliance with the Eastmans and his vocal distrust of Klein, Paul cheerfully signed both agreements. Indeed, though the Northern Songs fight dragged on interminably—and though the Beatles would eventually lose it—they were as unified during the summer of 1969 as they would ever be.

Taking advantage of the moment, Paul got them back into the studio once more. This time, things flowed so smoothly that *Abbey Road* was recorded faster than any album since *Help!* It also had the entire group playing ensemble on most of the tracks, and the vocal cuts are Beatle harmonies rather than a single vocalist's overdubs. Though it contains only the usual quota of Harrison songs, one of them—"Something"—was actually released as the A-side of a single and became a monster hit. Everything, for the first time since Brian's death, seemed to be going right. And then John made his announcement: "I want a divorce." He was, he said, bored.

There is never an adequate answer to that statement, and with Paul's stunned acceptance of the fact, the Beatles were dead. They all agreed to keep the divorce a secret, however, perhaps hoping that the rift could somehow be patched up.

But the fans were less worried about the demise of the Beatles than the death of Paul. The rumor seems to have begun in Detroit, where a local FM station pushed the story hard, and where the *Michigan Daily* ran an "obituary" review of *Abbey Road*. Clues abounded: On the cover of *Abbey Road*, Paul is barefoot and out of step with the others, his cigarette is in the wrong hand, and the license plate on the parked Volkswagen reads 28 IF—Paul's age *if* he had lived.

And that was only the beginning; other crazed truth-seekers found evidence of a bloody traffic accident on November 9th, 1966, which, of course, explained why the band had stopped touring and had buried themselves in recording studios where they could disguise Paul's absence with electronic trickery. So great was the demand for evidence that *Sgt. Pepper* (and even *Magical Mystery Tour*) reappeared on the album charts, and Capitol Records reported that the Beatles were en-joying the greatest monthly sales in their history. Not surprisingly, Capitol did nothing to dispel the rumors.

Paul was, however, very much alive (and only twenty-seven, as it happened). He had built a recording studio in his Scottish home, where he and Linda were busy recording an album; he played all the instruments, and she contributed vocal harmonies. Shortly before it was released (at almost the same time as *Let It Be*, the abandoned "roots" album), he confirmed his existence by publicly announcing he was quitting the Beatles.

By taking it on himself to betray their pledge of silence, Paul was obviously reaping some publicity benefits, but that is too cynical a view to serve as a complete explanation for his action. He had struggled hardest to keep them together, and there is something right in his shouldering the pain of finally parting them.

And there's no doubt he felt pain. Even in doomed affairs, there is often desperate ambivalence at parting. One person—to escape the relationship and be sure of never coming back—is finally driven to a cruelty that proves love still exists. Love doesn't make for clean breaks, but messy fractures.

Paul splintered bone in one of the questions he chose to ask himself in the "interview" packaged with his solo album. In any other context, it would be simply mean; remembering their music, it is tragic.

Q: "Did you miss the other Beatles and George Martin? Was there a moment, e.g., when you thought 'Wish Ringo was here for this break?'"

A: "No." □

CREDITS

(Pages 2-3) Popperfoto; (9) top, Popperfoto; (10) top, Popperfoto; (13) Black Star; (21) Astrid Kirchherr /Camera Press; (25) Keystone; (29) top, Astrid Kirchherr; (32-33) Keystone; (34) London Express /Pictorial Parade; (35, 36-37) Keystone; (38) Robert Freeman; (39) top, Keystone; bottom, Robert Freeman; (40, 41, 42, 43) Robert Freeman; (44-45) Keystone; (45) top, Syndication International /Photo Trends; (46) Robert Freeman; (48-49) Keystone; (50) top, bottom and (50-51) Robert Freeman; (51) top, Photo Trends; (51) bottom, Robert Freeman; (52-53) Robert Freeman; (54-55) Keystone; (55, 56-57) London Express /Pictorial Parade; (59) Photo Trends; (60-61) Associated Newspapers / Pictorial Parade; (61) Syndication International /Photo Trends; (62, 63) Terence Spencer /Life Magazine ©1964 Time Inc.; (64-64-65) London Express /Pictorial Parade; (72) Julian Wasser /Life Magazine ©Time Inc.; (72-73) Popperfoto; (74-75, 75, 76-77) Bill Eppridge /Life Magazine ©1964 Time Inc.; (78) Arthur Schatz /Life Magazine ©Time Inc.; (79) London Express /Pictorial Parade; (80-81) Bill Eppridge /Life Magazine ©Time Inc.; (82-83) Dezo Hoffmann; (83) Toby Massey /Miami Daily News / Photo Trends; (84) Dezo Hoffmann; (86, 87) Wide World; (88, 89) Bill Eppridge /Life Magazine ©Time Inc.; (90-91) Charles L. Trainor /Miami News; (92-93) Bill Eppridge /Life Magazine ©Time Inc.; (94) London Express /Pictorial Parade; (94-95) Bob Gomel /Life Magazine ©Time Inc.; (96) Syndication International /Photo Trends; (97) Charles L. Trainor /Miami News; (98-99, 100, 101) Bob Gomel /Life Magazine ©Time Inc.; (102) Charles L. Trainor /Miami News /Photo Trends; (103, 104-105) Charles L. Trainor /Miami News; (106-107) Robert Freeman; (108-109) Keystone; (110) Syndication International /Photo Trends; (111) United Artists; (112, 112-113, 114-115) Syndication International /Photo Trends; (116) top, Culver Pictures; bottom, London Express /Pictorial Parade; (117) top, London Express /Pictorial Parade; bottom, Pictorial Parade; (118) Syndication International /Photo Trends; (119) John Launois /Camera Press; (120, 121) London Express /Pictorial Parade; (122) Keystone; (123, 124-125, 125) London Express /Pictorial Parade; (126-127) Syndication International /Photo Trends; (128) Popperfoto; (128-129) Camera Press /Photo Trends; (130) Syndication International /Photo Trends; (131, 132, 133) London Express / Pictorial Parade; (136, 137) Frank Edwards /Fotos International; (138) Syndication International /Photo Trends; (138-139) Wide World; (140-141) Syndication International /Photo Trends; (141) Black Star; (142) Theo Bergstrom /Camera Press; (143) Robert Freeman; (144) Central Press /Pictorial Parade; (145) Popperfoto; (146) United Artists; (146-147) Syndication International /Photo Trends; (148) top, London Express /Pictorial Parade; bottom, Culver Pictures; (149) top, Culver Pictures; bottom, Popperfoto; (150) UPI; (151) Bob Whittaker /Keystone; (152-153) Wide World; (152) bottom, Peter Simon; (153) bottom, Keystone; (154) London Express /Pictorial Parade; (155) Keystone; (156) Black Star; (157) Syndication International /Photo Trends; (158-159) London Express /Pictorial Parade; (161) Central Press /Pictorial Parade; (162) top, Syndication International /Photo Trends; bottom, Camera Press; (163) Photo Trends; (164-165) London Express /Pictorial Parade; (165) top, London Express /Pictorial Parade; bottom, Popperfoto; (166) T. Tanuma /Life Magazine ©1966 Time Inc.; (166-167) Camera Press; (168, 169, 170-171) T. Tanuma /Life Magazine ©1966 Time Inc.; (172) top, Keystone; bottom, London Express /Pictorial Parade; (173) UPI; (174, 175, 176, 177, 178, 179) Keystone; (180) Syndication International /Photo Trends; (181) Popperfoto; (182) Marvin Lichtner /Life Magazine ©Time Inc.; (184-185) Fox Photos; (186) Syndication International /Photo Trends; (187) top, Camera Press /Photo Trends; bottom, Central Press /Pictorial Parade; (188-189) Keystone; (190) top, Popperfoto; bottom, Keystone; (191) Keystone; (194-195) Keystone; (195) Syndication International /Photo Trends; (196) London Express /Pictorial Parade; (196-197, 198, 199, 200, 201, 202-203, 203, 205) Keystone; (206) Paris Match /Pictorial Parade; (206-207) Lazzaro Franchetti /Liaison; (208) Syndication International /Photo Trends; (209) Linda Eastman; (211) Ringo Starr; (212) London Express /Pictorial Parade; (213) Central Press / Pictorial Parade; (216) Syndication International /Photo Trends; (217) John Lennon /Photo Trends; (218-219) Popperfoto; (219) top, Popperfoto; bottom, Tom Blau /Camera Press; (220) Jeremy Banks /Camera Press; (220-221) Stephen Goldblatt /Photo Trends; (222) top, Bruce McBroom /Camera Press; bottom, Stephen Goldblatt /Camera Press; (224-225, 225) Stephen Goldblatt /Camera Press; (226) top, Tom Hanley /Photo Trends; bottom, United Artists; (227) Linda Eastman; (228) United Artists; (228-229) London Express /Pictorial Parade; (230) Popperfoto; (231) Syndication International /Photo Trends; (232) London Express /Pictorial Parade; (233) UPI; (234-235) Bruce McBroom /Camera Press; (240, 241, 242, 243) Ethan A. Russell /Photo Trends.

Editor: Mary Gimbel
Managing Editor: Audrey Berman
Photo Research: Stephanie Franklin
Editorial Research: Pauline Finkelstein
Assistance: Malu Halasa, Debra Hurst,
Elaine Long, John Rea,
Vincent Schmelzkopf, Martine Winter

Consultant: Marianne Partridge
Designed by Bea Feitler and Carl Barile

Cover design by Andy Warhol, ©1980
Photographs by Dezo Hoffmann

The text is set in monotype Centaur by Mackenzie-Harris of
San Francisco, with display in Corvinus Skyline
and Arrighi by Artintype Metro and M. J. Baumwell of New York.
Printed by the web offset process by Krueger.